The Whole *Megilla*

The Whole *Megilla*

Reading the Tractate on the *Scroll of Esther* in the Babylonian Talmud

Joshua A. Fogel

HAMILTON BOOKS
an imprint of
Rowman & Littlefield
Lanham • Boulder • New York • London

Published by Hamilton Books
An imprint of The Rowman & Littlefield Publishing Group, Inc.
4501 Forbes Boulevard, Suite 200, Lanham, Maryland 20706
www.rowman.com
86-90 Paul Street, London EC2A 4NE, United Kingdom

Copyright © 2022 by The Rowman & Littlefield Publishing Group, Inc.

All rights reserved. No part of this book may be reproduced in any form or by any electronic or mechanical means, including information storage and retrieval systems, without written permission from the publisher, except by a reviewer who may quote passages in a review.

British Library Cataloguing in Publication Information Available

Library of Congress Cataloging-in-Publication Data Available

ISBN 978-0-7618-7364-8 (pbk.) | ISBN 978-0-7618-7365-5 (ebook)

To my daughters, Antigone and Avital

Contents

Introduction	ix
Chapter 1: Reading the *Megilla*	1
Chapter 2: Properly Reading the *Megilla*	69
Chapter 3: Rules for Reading the *Megilla* and the Torah	87
Chapter 4: Laws of the Synagogue and Torah Readings	109
Glossary of Selected Terms	133
General Index	135
Biblical and Rabbinic References Index	141
About the Author	143

Introduction

Many people have expounded on the Merkava *[chariot in Ezekiel's vision], although they have never seen it.* (24b)

While the holiday of Purim (lit., lots) is not considered a major holiday, it remains enormously popular. The story as recounted in the *Scroll of Esther* (*megilla* means scroll) dates back to an era between the destruction of the first Temple and the construction of the second one. It is a tale of the plot by the "evil Haman" (*Haman harasha*) to exterminate the Jewish people who are saved in the eleventh hour by God—and the name of God is famously not mentioned even once throughout the text. The fact that God's intervention to save the Jewish people is not explicit has been interpreted to indicate that this miracle is qualitatively different from other miracles He performed which are explicit in the Torah. Because of this difference, then, publicizing the miracle—otherwise not apparent—becomes all the more important. This is the background for why Purim is probably the most exuberant of Jewish holiday celebrations. Indeed, the Jewish people are commanded to get drunk, so drunk in fact that one cannot distinguish the hero of the story (Mordechai) from the villain (Haman).

Haman has been variously conceived as a descendant of Amalek and a forerunner of Adolf Hitler, in that all three wished to exterminate the entire Jewish people and all were ultimately unsuccessful. The story is set in the Persian court of the utterly clueless King Achashverosh (Xerxes I) who is prodded into taking action in the nick of time against his evil vizier (Haman) who pays the final price at the end of the *Scroll* along with his ten sons. One oddity of the story not much spoken of among the religious authorities is the fact that it also celebrates the intermarriage of this king with a Jewish woman, Esther, who is the heroine of the *Scroll* named for her. Well, it is not as though Esther displayed any agency in her choice of spouse; she had no opportunity to refuse, as monarchs tend to do as they wish, and the king selected her for her great beauty. The Talmudic tractate goes to great lengths, as we shall see, to indirectly deal with this otherwise religiously unsanctioned practice of intermarriage.

The tractate *Megilla* only begins with the text of the *Megilla* itself, and like so many (if not all) other tractates, moves off in many directions to explicate the text of the *Scroll* and many tangential issues as well, as we shall see. Roughly half the text concerns matters unrelated or at best obliquely related to the holiday of Purim. Some of these issues are technical—when precisely is the *Scroll of Esther* read in synagogue, as it is a religious requirement that all Jews at least hear the *Scroll* read each year in its unique chant—and some are much more homiletical. It is the prototypical holiday for the joke that so many Jewish holidays commemorate: we were about to be exterminated, God saved us, let's eat. The commandment to feast is the root of the practice of delivering portions of food or sweets to friends and to the poor (Hebrew, *mishloach manot*; Yiddish, *shalakhmones*). In fact, Jews are commanded to be so festive that no eulogies are permitted on Purim.

Most of the latter half of this tractate deals with general holiday and Sabbath practices: which portions of the Torah are to be read on which holidays or fast days, which additional readings (from the Prophets and Writings) are to be read when, how many people on such days are to be called to read, and the like. There are even more general issues raised about the sale of an old synagogue which leads to lengthy disquisitions on the implications of the broader dictum that "in matters of holiness, we only raise but do not lower."

A NOTE ON THE TALMUD ITSELF

In the world's most commonly used edition, the Babylonian Talmud fills 2,711 folio pages or 5,422 ordinary, contemporary pages. It is composed of the Mishna and the Gemara; the former categorizing and commenting on numerous topics under the heading of each tractate and the latter the rabbis of the early centuries following the destruction of the Temple in 70 CE. Some of the material continues to inform daily and festival life for observant and even semi-observant Jews around the globe, as is certainly the case with the celebration of Purim. Yet, much of the material concerns a world that ceased to exist with the destruction in 70 CE of the second Temple in Jerusalem, including offerings brought to the Temple and sacrificed there, the Temple's structure and layout, levirate marriage, punishments for a host of transgressions, tithing regulations, and the like.

Over the course of the centuries, students began to study only those tractates of the Talmud that interested them or their teachers to the neglect of other tractates, meaning oftentimes that certain tractates were ignored. In

1923, Rabbi Meir Shapiro (1887–1933), born into a long line of Hassidic rabbis in Romania and soon to become the rabbi of Lublin, Poland, came up with a solution. He suggested an elaborate plan to read one *daf* (folio page; plural, *dapim*) each day in orderly fashion, replicated everywhere that people studied Talmud on a regular basis; this is known as the *daf yomi* (one folio per day) cycle. It was to take roughly seven years and five months to complete a cycle. He proposed his plan on August 16 at the First World Congress of the international Agudath Israel in Vienna, and it was soon accepted and put into practice on September 11, 1923 (Rosh Hashanah). At a ceremony celebrating the completion (*siyum*) of the most recent (thirteenth) cycle, over 90,000 people gathered at the Metlife Stadium in New Jersey.

As is the case with all tractates of the Babylonian Talmud, we begin with folio 2 (there is no folio 1). We shall be offering both summaries and explanations to the extent possible of each folio, recto (a) and verso (b). There are four chapters of uneven length in this tractate: One runs from 2a through 17a; Two from 17a to 21a; Three from 21a to 25b; and Four from 25b to 32a. There is a glossary of technical terms at the back for easy reference, as necessary.

Chapter 1

Reading the *Megilla*

This chapter begins with a discussion of when (dates and times) we read the *Scroll of Esther* (H. *Megillat Esther*) in different places. It moves on to the customary practices associated with commemoration of the holiday. And, as it frequently does, it strays into freely associated and somewhat tangential (even unrelated) topics along the way. There is much *aggada* (homiletic elucidation) in this chapter. Buckle your seatbelts.

2a

The first Mishna begins by stating precisely when we are to read the *Scroll of Esther*, and it demonstrates by example why one often needs help with the Talmudic text. We are to read it on Adar 11, or Adar 12, or (perhaps) Adar 13, 14, or 15 (usually, in February-March)—but not earlier or later. This will take some clarification. The first clarification states that we read it on the fifteenth in cities that had walls in the time of Joshua, most prominently Shushan, the Persian capital and scene of the action in the *Scroll*. Larger towns and villages (without walls in Joshua's day) read it on the fourteenth, and villages are allowed to read it or, more likely, hear it read, even earlier when local courts were in session (Mondays and Thursdays). If Adar 14 happens to fall on a Monday, then problem solved for villagers, while those in walled cities wait and read it the next day. If, however, Adar 14 happens to fall on a Tuesday or Wednesday, villagers do the reading on the preceding Monday (Adar 13 or 12, respectively), when the courts are in session; those in large towns read the *Scroll* that very day, and those in walled cities the next day, Adar 15. If Adar 14 falls on a Thursday, villagers and those in larger towns read it that day, while walled city residents wait until Friday. If it should fall on a Friday, however, villagers read it the day before, while those in large towns and walled cities stick with Friday.

No one, however, is to read the *Scroll* on Shabbat. This last measure predates the institutionalization of a fixed calendar devised by Hillel II in 359

CE, such that Adar 14 can never fall on Shabbat. Before that, should Adar 14 fall on a Saturday, villagers and those in large towns move their reading back to Thursday, the most recent day of assembly, while walled city residents push the reading forward to Sunday, Adar 15. We've covered Adar 12–15 for possible reading days. What about the very first allowable date, Adar 11? The last sentence of our Mishna explains that, if Adar 14 falls on a Sunday, villagers read the *Scroll* on the most recent assembly day: Thursday, Adar 11; those in large towns read it that very day, and walled city residents wait until Monday, Adar 15.

So, interestingly, that first sentence of our Mishna doesn't, as it might appear, offer us a smorgasbord of dates from which to choose when we might like to read the *Scroll*. It lays out the possibilities and then details the circumstances surrounding those five possible dates.

As is its wont, the Gemara begins by citing snippets from the Mishna and then launching into explanatory commentary. The *Scroll of Esther* makes provisions for us to read it on Adar 14 or 15, as we have seen, but how, asks the Gemara, can we extend that back three more days? This time the answer is fairly simple. Wise men were doing villagers a favor. The latter group provided urbanites with food and water for the Purim feast; by allowing a reading on an earlier assembly day (Monday or Thursday), that meant they would be back in their villages and able to service the needs of city dwellers.

The Gemara goes even further now, stating that the Men of the Great Assembly (of which Mordechai was allegedly a member, 120 members in all; see *Ethics of the Father*) must have allowed these earlier possible dates, or later sages would never have been in any position to make such a unilateral determination. This statement allows the Gemara to issue an important general ruling: no court can overrule the judgment of another court unless it wiser or larger in number of members. It goes without saying that the "Great Assembly" gained that name for a reason, as no court was ever as wise. Nonetheless, the Men of the Great Assembly (who composed the *Scroll*) cannot have made a ruling out of thin air, so they must have discerned a reason for permitting Adar 11–13 for reading the *Scroll*. The Gemara proceeds to tease it out.

First up is Rav Shemen bar Abba, citing R. Yochanan who was his teacher incidentally, and he suggests that a superfluous word in the *Scroll* concerning the date of Purim might mean that Adar 14 and 15 were not the only ones. The word here meaning "their times" is in the plural which the Gemara usually takes to mean two. The Gemara merciless dispenses with this suggestion by categorically stating that the term in question was not superfluous and did in fact refer to two times (Adar 14 and 15). But, one must quickly grow a thick skin in the give-and-take of Talmudic debate, and Rav Shemen's argument strikes back and apparently wins the day by reading into the letters of the word in question.

Yet, does it? Yes, we now can assert that readings outside walled cities may take place on days other than Adar 14 or 15, but why are Adar 11–13 the only other possibilities? What's wrong with Adar 1–10, for example? It has to be one of two days, not one of ten or more. Adar 11–13 is three days, and the Gemara does some fancy footwork to eliminate Adar 13 as needing special mention; so, the two days are Adar 11–12. And, before one has time to even think it, the Gemara rules out dates in Adar after the fifteenth, as the *Scroll* (9.27) rules against going beyond Adar 15. R. Shmuel bar Nachmani offers a different analysis to come up with the same answer. And, if that's not enough, the Gemara asks why R. Shmuel did not use Rav Shemen's logic and why Rav Shemen did not use R. Shmuel's.

One of the immediate problems raised by the foregoing is that our ancestors established the date for Passover as thirty days following the reading of the *Scroll* (usually dating from Adar 14). When the Jewish people ruled in the Land of Israel, the court in Jerusalem established the dates in advance, such as when there would be leap years and the like. Runners from the capital would notify people in outlying villages as to when months would begin, and thus dating the holidays was relatively easy. After the destruction of the Temple and the dispersion, however, this system of notification was no longer tenable, and to ensure that Passover was properly observed in its time, Adar 14 was established as the earliest date for Purim's reading of the *Scroll of Esther*.

R. Yehuda was the author of this argument, namely that villagers no longer have the leeway to fix their reading before Adar 14, and the Gemara claims that this is a thorough rejection of the position of R. Yochanan. Although this is the *halacha* (Jewish law), when is a rejection not really a complete rejection? The Gemara will not let R. Yochanan's view disappear so easily. Rav Ashi finds an internal contradiction in R. Yehuda's argument.

2b

The thrust of Rav Ashi's dispute is to say that, even now with our people dispersed in many far-flung places, still the Gemara's dispensation to villages to read the *Scroll* before Adar 14 holds. This issue promises to crop up in a few *dapim*, so we shall table it for now.

The Gemara next takes up the Mishna's statement about residents of walled cities in the time of Joshua having to read the *Scroll* on Adar 15. Again, the Gemara wants to know where that dating comes from—that is, why the fifteenth, given that the verse in the text of the *Scroll* allows for either Adar 14 or 15. Rava provides an extremely simple response. Our text stipulates that residents of "unwalled" cities are to read the *Scroll* on Adar 14; thus, that must mean that Adar 15 is for their coreligionists in walled cities. But, yes, this is not only extremely simple, but the Gemara avers that it is too simple. For, if residents of unwalled cities have Adar 14 to celebrate Purim, perhaps those in cities with walls can pass on the holiday altogether. The Gemara, needless to say, discards this out of hand, as the *Scroll* states plainly that Jews throughout Achashverosh's kingdom were obliged without question to celebrate the holiday.

So, the Gemara attempts another approach. If people in unwalled cities do indeed celebrate the holiday on Adar 14, perhaps their confreres in walled cities could do the same on either Adar 14 or 15. The text of the *Scroll* (9.21) seems to offer this option; in fact, the wording seems to imply that it is a two-day holiday. Now, to disabuse us of this possibility, the Gemara reads into the grammar of the *Scroll*'s phrasing. By repeating the Hebrew object particle *et*, we are told, the text is effectively telling us the Adar 14 is for unwalled cities and Adar 15 for walled cities. This reasoning may strike readers as a bit of a stretch, but it is highly typical of the manner in which the Gemara often employs grammar and (as we have seen above) the actual letters (or lack of them) in words to draw bigger conclusions. The "logic" here is that there is nothing in sacred texts (and nothing purposefully omitted) that are accidental, and we shall certainly see more of this in what follows.

Another run at the way the dating has been derived: perhaps, yes, Adar 14 is for unwalled cities, but residents of walled cities might be able to choose between Adar 14 and 15. Of course, this won't fly any better than its predecessors, but it must be raised if only to be discarded. The rationale here is that each of these two dates have their own distinctive "times," and thus the twain shall not meet. One further possibility is raised and dismissed.

Almost in passing, the Gemara notes that this dating specifically refers to our celebration of the holiday, not to the reading of the *Scroll*, but this is dispensed with pronto, for the *Scroll of Esther* (9.28) states: "These days [of Purim; namely the 14th or 15th of Adar] are to be commemorated and celebrated." So, we do both, celebrating and reading, on the appointed day(s).

R. Yehoshua ben Korcha is now cited about the business of walled cities in Joshua's day. He thinks the standard should be that people in walled cities at the time of Achashverosh read the *Scroll* on Adar 15. His reason is a bit circular; namely, at that time in Shushan, itself a walled city, they read the *Scroll* on the fifteenth, so that should set the norm. The Tanna (namely the sage who is leading the argument against all "assailants") rebuffs this assault with a *gezera shava*, one of the thirteen hermeneutic tools of the Talmud; that is by citing, usually, two instances of the same word in the Torah and making inferences from one to the other (sometimes, as here, one of those two instances is not from Torah but from either the Prophets or Writings, and this can ruffle sagely feathers). The word in question, *perazi* (unwalled towns) is mentioned in the *Scroll*, and in *Deuteronomy* (3.5) it refers to such a place when Joshua was conquering the Land of Israel. Therefore, Joshua is our guy. R. Yehoshua ben Korcha, though, doesn't abide by this *gezera shava*.

Now, the Gemara throws a question back at our Tanna. Shushan celebrated the festival on Adar 15, but did Shushan have a wall in the time of Joshua? Can we even know this for certain? Rava plays a little fast and loose in responding that Shushan is exceptional because it was home to the miracle of Purim, and his subsequent explanation strikes this author as a little thin. A longer discussion ensues about what constitutes a walled or unwalled town, and that the terrain beyond the walls of the former belongs to the town when it comes to setting a date for Purim. Needless to say, the Gemara asks for greater clarity about how close to a walled city does the land have to be to "belong" to it for halachic purposes. Answer: one *mil* (roughly two-thirds to three-quarters of a mile).

This last teaching about distance was brought to us by R. Yirmeya, though some believe it have been R. Chiyya bar Abba. So, the Gemara uses this opportunity, as it often does, to segue into another teaching by R. Yirmeya (or R. Chiyya bar Abba) which bears at best a tangential relationship to the question at hand—actually, it's unrelated altogether. He claims that the final forms of six Hebrew letters, which differ from them when they appear elsewhere in a word, were instituted by the Prophets. Now, the Gemara will have none of this, for the Torah's commandments were sealed after the revelation at Sinai, thus making it impossible for the Prophets to give them any new graphic forms. Rav Chisda notes here that the final *mem* (which resembles a square) was right there in the Tablets with which Moses returned from the mountain, meaning that at least that final letter long predated the Prophets.

3a

The Gemara now tries to have it both way by agreeing that the form of these letters that now appear at the end of words did indeed exist long before the Prophets appeared on the scene, but saying that until that time people didn't know which forms appeared at the end and which elsewhere in words—the Prophets cleared all that up. Yet, as the Gemara points out, back on *daf* 2b, Leviticus 27.34 ("these are the commandments") is cited, and it clearly rules out the Prophets making any changes of the sort just suggested. The response is dubious at best: the proper placement of the proper forms of letters was forgotten after having been instituted in Moses' time, and the Prophets corrected all that.

As long as we're spinning off on an aside from R. Yirmeya (or R. Chiyya bar Abba), the Gemara offers another, this time on "translation" (*targum*) of Scripture into Aramaic. Of the famous *targum* of the Torah done by Onkeles (the convert), we learn that he acquired knowledge of it from R. Eliezer and R. Yehoshua; and the *targum* of the Prophets was the work of Yonatan ben Uziel who acquired it from three late Prophets. The last of these is, of course, impossible as Yonatan lived many years after the Prophets, but the implication is that by a chain of teachers it was passed down to him. One would now think that this an extraordinarily positive achievement, as Hebrew had lost most of its currency and Aramaic was the *lingua franca* of the Jewish people. However, with the completion of Yonatan's work, the Land of Israel experienced something like an earthquake, and a Heavenly Voice (*bat kol*) rang out demanding to know who had had the chutzpah to make the "secrets" of God's word available to "humankind" (*bnei adam*). Yonatan fesses up and assumes that the invisible author of the *bat kol* is, indeed, God—although, one has to ask here, why would an omniscient God need to ask such a question, meaning that this would have to have been a rhetorical question. He explains that he did what he did not for any personal or familial honor but for the glory of God and so that differences of understanding the Lord's word would cease now that everyone was on the same *daf*, so to speak.

When Yonatan reveals that he'd also like to prepare a *targum* of the Writings, God rings out another *bat kol*: "You've done enough" (*dayecha*). The Gemara wants to know what's up with that. Why prevent the Writings from being translated into Aramaic so that humankind will have a much easier time understanding their contents. This isn't posed as a question from Yonatan to God, but the Gemara just answers its own question by stating that there is an allusion in one of the texts of the Writings to the coming of the Messiah at the end of days (from *Daniel*). No explanation is offered, but one assumes that this was seen to be too heady for ordinary humans to handle.

The Gemara next turns to Onkeles's rendering of the Torah. It then gives us a passage from the prophet Nehemiah, not because it immediately explains everything but as a text to clarify the importance of Onkeles's work. It then takes this sentence apart almost word-for-word to elucidate how it perfectly explains the import of Onkeles's *targum*, right down to the trope symbols indicating how the reader of Torah inflects his voice, a system invented many years after Onkeles's time. We have a problem, though, inasmuch as Nehemiah lived centuries before Onkeles, but the Gemara uses the same evasive maneuver it did with the question of forms of Hebrew letters: Onkeles didn't actually write the *targum*; it long preceded him, but was forgotten and he somehow revived it.

What was it about the Prophets *targum* that caused an earthquake? Why was Onkeles's work not equally earth-shaking? The answer is rather simple:

The Torah is straightforward in meaning, no secrets to speak of. However, the Prophets do, in fact, touch occasionally on secretive material, and their revelation to wider humankind deserved a *bat kol*. What's an example of such a secret that the *targum* made manifest in Aramaic? The Gemara is glad you asked. It refers us to a passage in *Zechariah* in which the original text is unclear, but the *targum* explicates with references to the books of *Kings*.

You might be forgiven at this point if you've forgotten that this tractate of the Talmud is allegedly about the *Megilla*, but that's just how the Talmud rolls. We return now to another ruling by either R. Yirmeya or R. Chiyya bar Abba. A passage is cited from the book of *Daniel* (10.7) in which he reports of a vision which the folks with him did not see; nonetheless, those other people were overcome with fear and ran away. So who were those other guys? R. Yirmeya (or R. Chiyya) claim that it must have been the three prophets Chaggai, Zechariah, and Malachi. Seems odd, inasmuch as they were full-fledged prophets, but Daniel outranked them in having seen this vision. Yet, if they failed to see what Daniel had seen, why did they run scared? Well, uh, apparently their "guardian angels" did see it and inspired their escape, though we still do not know what frightened these angels. So, if one becomes alarmed but doesn't know why, he is advised to recite the *Shema* passages from the Torah (*Deuteronomy* 6.4–9, 11.13–21; *Numbers* 15.37–41); should he find himself at such a frightened point in time standing in a filthy place where one is admonished never to recite the *Shema*, he is advised to move four paces away. For those unable to move away, there is an epithet he can enunciate.

Now, we finally return to the *Scroll* (9.28), and the Gemara asks what the phrase "family and family" (regarding celebrating the holiday) refers to. R. Yose bar Chanina tells us that this points to the families of the Kohanim (priests) and Levites who are to leave their Temple services when it's time for the reading of the *Scroll of Esther*. Most authorities deem that the latter takes precedence over sacrificial services in the Temple. Ordinarily, the Kohanim would have been performing their duties with musical accompaniment from the Levites and also in attendance a representative group of Israelites. When it was time to read the *Megilla*, all would abandon their stations to go and hear it read. We learn at this point that the school of one of the greatest of ancient rabbis, R. Yehuda ha-Nasi (Rabbi Judah the Prince, 135–220) who is usually referred to in the Talmud simple as "Rabbi," claims that one must also abandon Torah study to go hear the *Megilla*. They reason by means of another of the thirteen hermeneutic principles, this one called *kal vachomer* (lit., light and heavy; implying lenient and stringent). If abandoning the Temple service is required to hear the *Megilla*, then certainly something less stringent— namely, Torah study—must also be also be abandoned.

But, wait, is the study of Torah a more lenient commandment than the Temple's sacrificial service? Teaching by example, the Gemara refers us to R. Yehoshua ben Levi who cites a passage from the book of his namesake *Joshua* in which the latter confronts an angel near the city of Jericho. What is this all about, one may well wonder. The angel announces to Joshua that he (Joshua) has both failed to offer the afternoon sacrifice and failed to study Torah that day. To be sure, Joshua was leading an army in war and was technically exempt from Torah study.

3b

Joshua immediately hunkered down to study Torah.

We're now ready to hone in on a proof. Drawing on the same passage from *Joshua*, Rav Shmuel bar Unya claims that Joshua's angel only appeared when he neglected study of Torah, which means that abandonment of the Temple service was of less immediate concern. This would challenge the statement of the school of R. Yehuda ha-Nasi. And, now the Talmud pulls a trick out of its bag that it frequently does to demonstrate that both sides of this dispute may be right. How so? In the incident involving Joshua, all of the Israelites had ignored their study of Torah which meant it transcended abandonment of the daily sacrifices, whereas the essence of the school of R. Yehuda ha-Nasi was that an individual's Torah study was less important than those same sacrificial services. The Gemara next cites a passage in another tractate concerning what one may or may not do when a Torah scholar dies on certain holidays, including Purim, in order to distinguish between the stringency of venerating such an individual versus the more lenient matter of an individual's study of Torah.

Rava then refers us back to *daf* 3a and approving cites R. Yose bar Chanina to deem that hearing the reading of the *Megilla* trumps Temple service; he then approves as well the ruling of R. Yehuda ha-Nasi's school that the *Megilla* reading trumps individual Torah study. He continues with a comparison to the duties of Torah study versus burying a corpse who has no relative present—the latter takes precedence. Covering all options, Rava now compares relative obligations between sacrificial service and corpse burial; the latter again takes precedence. The reasoning here involves creative reading of scriptural texts. Thus far, Rava has elaborated fairly straightforward cases. What, then, about a potential conflict between hearing the *Scroll* read and burial of a corpse? The *Scroll* could come first because it publicly announces the miracle God performed to save the Jewish people; or, maybe burying a corpse is deemed primary because of the issue of human dignity involved. Rava goes with the burial option on the basis of the extreme importance of the issue of human dignity, something that has the capacity to cause a deferral of a prohibition of the Torah. Inasmuch as reading the *Megilla* is only a rabbinical duty, it steps aside in the face of burial.

The Gemara now returns to an issue it dealt with on the previous *daf*. According to R. Yehoshua ben Levi, we are to understand "walled city" to mean that city, everything "near" it, and everything that can be "seen" from it. On Adar 15, the entire region then celebrates Purim. A unwalled city "near" but not visible from a walled city is considered like that walled city, and an unwalled city that can been "seen" from the walled city even if it is not "near" is also considered like the walled city. The latter strikes the Gemara as fully possible, such as an unwalled city atop a mountain, but the former case seems difficult. R. Yirmeya explains it by flipping the scene: if the unwalled city is in a valley.

R. Yehoshua ben Levi has some other thoughts as well. A settlement with homes which subsequently built a surrounding wall is considered an unwalled city for purposes of the *Megilla*, citing a passage in *Leviticus* (25.29). If the wall was built first, that would be a different case. Another teaching from the same rabbi: any city lacking ten idle men always in synagogue to constitute a *minyan* for various communal purposes is considered a village. The Gemara notes immediately that this last point is covered in the Mishna (5a), but R. Yehoshua ben Levi was referring to a city, whereas the Mishna will be discussing a town. On a roll, R. Yehoshua ben Levi goes on to state that a walled city that was demolished and later settled by people is considered a walled city. The Gemara wants a little more precision on what is meant by "demolished"; if that means the walls were destroyed and settlement ensued (meaning rebuilt walls), then indeed it is a walled city, but if no settlement ensued, then it does not rise to walled city status. R. Eliezer bar Yose cites a line from *Leviticus* to the effect that any city that once had a wall is considered as if it still does at present. And, R. Yehoshua ben Levi's point, according to the Gemara, is that demolition here must be referring to the lack of return of its group of ten idle men.

The Gemara goes on with more teachings of R. Yehoshua ben Levi on the next *daf*.

4a

He asserts that three cities—Lod (Lydda), Ono, and Gei Hecharashim—did indeed have walls in Joshua's time. The Gemara, though, seems doubtful, citing a passage from *I Chronicles* stating that it was Elpaal who built Lod and Ono (no mention of Gei Hecharashim). And, if that's not enough, there is circumstantial evidence that it was Asa, a king of Judah, who built these cities much later. R. Elazar saves the day by getting the history right and preserving R. Yehoshua ben Levi's initial assertion: these cities did, indeed, have walls in Joshua's era; they were destroyed and rebuilt by Elpaal; and they collapsed once again and were refortified by Asa.

Another from R. Yehoshua ben Levi, and this one is a really interesting one. He claims that taking part in the reading of the *Scroll of Esther* is an obligation incumbent upon women as well as men, because they were encompassed in the miracle that the holiday commemorates. No complaints or disagreements are registered here by the Gemara. Ordinarily, women are excepted from time-bound, positive commandments, but because they were explicitly among those Haman sought to wipe out (*Esther* 3.13) or possible because Esther was the vehicle through which the miracle came to pass, they must also partake of the reading. This doesn't necessarily mean that they can read the *Scroll* with men in synagogue, though some authorities do indeed sanction that.

What happens when Purim lands on Shabbat? R. Yehoshua ben Levi lived after the institutionalization of the fixed calendar, so that by then Adar 14 could never fall on Shabbat. He must be referring to Adar 15. He states that on that Shabbat, in lieu of reading the *Scroll*, we need have lectures and the like to "publicize the miracle." But, the Gemara rhetorically replies, isn't this required on all Jewish holidays? However, R. Yehoshua ben Levi's teaching is necessary for a distinct reading. As we shall see shortly, Rabba rules that we should have no lectures about the *Scroll* on Shabbat, should Purim fall on that day, because people might voluntarily or involuntarily carry a copy of the *Megilla* more than four paces in the public domain, which it outlawed on Shabbat. R. Yehoshua ben Levi claims that Rabba's injunction is invalid.

Just one more for now: R. Yehoshua ben Levi states that we must read the *Megilla* on the night of Purim (Adar 14 in unwalled cities, Adar 15 in walled ones) and then repeat it the following morning. This ruling was seconded by R. Chiyya bar Abba who claims to have heard the ruling proclaimed in person. And, if that were not sufficient, R. Chelbo reiterates in the name of Ula Biraa the same teaching.

Now, the Gemara returns to explicating the Mishna, specifically the part about villagers on occasion celebrating the holiday earlier that Adar 14 or 15—on a previous Monday or Thursday, when people traditionally assemble. R. Chanina explains why this leniency was instituted, as explained on 2a.

4b

Challenges ensue. This leniency was to both enable the villagers to hear the *Megilla* reading and be back in their villages to provide food and water for the urbanites to enjoy the holiday. Now, what if the holiday falls on a Monday? The residents of villages and unwalled cities are instructed to read the *Megilla* then, but if the leniency was enacted so that the big city dwellers would be able to secure provisions for their celebration, shouldn't the reading for the villagers take place on the preceding Thursday (so they would be back in their homes, readying provisions for the urbanites)? No, resoundingly responds the Gemara, because that means their reading of the *Megilla* would be on Adar 10, and Sages of yore provided no such dispensation.

OK, but what if one year Adar 14 is a Thursday? The Mishna is clear that villagers and unwalled town residents read the *Megilla* that very day. By the same reasoning, shouldn't these folks read the *Megilla* on the preceding Monday and be back home readying food and water for the urbanites? That Monday would be Adar 11. This time there is a stark rebuttal: no shifting the reading of the *Scroll* from one day of assembly to another.

The Gemara finally cites a Mishna to which we shall come shortly in which R. Yehuda teaches that, while villagers who assemble in cities on Mondays and Thursday may indeed read the *Scroll* before Adar 14, what about those villagers who don't regularly assemble on those days? They are to read the *Scroll* on Adar 14, the prescribed date. That would indicate that this leniency is not explicitly for urbanites. Ultimately, then, the dispensation to villagers was not so that they would be *in situ* on Adar 14 to provide food and water to urbanites, but rather it was a concession to the villagers who thus need not make a special trip to local cities on Adar 14.

Back to the Mishna at hand where we read that, if Adar 14 turns out to be a Monday, all read the *Scroll* on that day. The Gemara starts on this piece of Mishna with an odd, if intriguing, question. Earlier in the Mishna it was talking about dates in the months of Adar (11 through 15), but why now is it talking about days of the week (Monday, Thursday, and the like)? The response is almost as odd: should the Gemara continue its references to dates of the month, it would perforce do so in reverse order which would be confusing—heaven knows that the Gemara is anything but confusing! In any event, the Tanna thus uses days of the week for clarity sake.

Back to the Mishna and its point about Adar 14 landing on Friday, when villagers read the *Scroll* on the preceding Thursday and city residents, with or without walls, on that Friday. Before getting into the weeds here, the Gemara basically warns us that we are entering a domain of not one, but two, clashes of views. So, who is the Tanna of this Mishna? There is a *baraita*, an oral tradition that didn't make it into the Mishna, that designates unwalled city residents to read the *Megilla* on Thursday, when the holiday falls on a Friday. R. Yehuda ha-Nasi disagrees, saying that these folks should read it on Friday, and thus his view corresponds with the Mishna's ruling, making him a prime candidate for our Tanna in question.

The Gemara now does something curious—it attempts to beef up the argument that we all know is going to go down in flames eventually. Why would the author of the *baraita* have made such a claim? Answer: the *Megilla* designates Adar 14 for people in unwalled towns, Adar 15 for those surrounded by walls; it also states explicitly that the holiday is to be celebrated "in its proper time each and every year" (*Esther* 9.27); so, if Adar 14 is a Friday, then perhaps both residents of cities with or without walls should move their dates of the reading one day back to keep the proper order. This is dispensed with by interpreting "each and every year" differently, affirming that that phrase necessitates that unwalled town read the *Megilla* on Adar 14, when it falls on Friday.

R. Yehuda ha-Nasi explains that residents of both sorts of cities read the *Megilla* on Friday, Adar 14, and his reasoning is word-for-word the same as outlined immediately above. The Gemara repeats the *baraita*'s reasoning that unwalled city's need precede walled cities in reading the *Megilla*. But, in the end R. Yehuda ha-Nasi's argument wins the day. And, that is a strong argument as well that he was the Tanna of our Mishna, but he has a contender.

Suppose the Tanna was actually R. Yose. The Gemara cites another *baraita* to which R. Yose will respond. This *baraita* begins like the previous one: if Adar 14 coincides with a Friday, meaning that walled cities cannot read the *Megilla* on Adar 15, but diverges by teaching that walled city residents and villagers then read it on Thursday, while unwalled city residents stick with Friday. R. Yose makes mincemeat out of this *baraita*. Walled cities can never precede unwalled ones! So, reverting to a Thursday while unwalled city resident follow on Friday makes no sense. When Adar 14 falls on Friday, residents of both types of cities read the *Megilla* that very day.

Again, the Gemara moves to bolster a view that is destined for oblivion. The *baraita* cites the same line from *Megilla*, "in each and every year," and claims that unwalled towns have no choice but celebrate on Adar 14, but (it claims) this date must differ from that on which walled cities celebrate. That means, it must be Adar 13 (Thursday), because it can't read the *Scroll* on Shabbat (Adar 15). The rebuttal comes quickly: walled cities, "each and every year," do not make a practice of reading the *Megilla* before unwalled ones. The hapless response is that walled cities can't read the *Megilla* on the same day as the unwalled one, because they need their own space. But, I say "hapless" because we know R. Yose is waiting in the wings to demolish this view.

R. Yose argues that, if Adar 15 is Shabbat, the both types of cities read the *Scroll* on Adar 14. "Each and every year" walled cities never precede unwalled ones. Thus, this instance is no exception to the rule. As we saw with the response at this point to R. Yehuda ha-Nasi, the last-minute support for the *baraita* claims that the two types of cities need their own separate days for reading the *Megilla*. R. Yose makes clear that, when we are faced with Adar 14 on Friday, there's no escaping both walled and unwalled cities from celebrating on that very day.

Before making a definitive ruling on the identity of the original Tanna of the Mishna here, the Gemara dredges up a *baraita* in the name of R. Yehuda ha-Nasi which sings a different tune. In that one, he rules that, if Adar 14 coincides with Shabbat, villagers celebrate on the preceding assembly day (Thursday), unwalled towns on Friday, and walled cities on the day after Shabbat (Sunday). Earlier we found him ruling that unwalled town residents read the *Megilla* on Friday, not swinging all the way back to an assembly day. Actually, the Gemara notes, these are not incompatible, for earlier Adar 14 fell on a Friday, and that meant all was fine for unwalled towns—no need to move their date for celebrating.

The Gemara inserts a query at this point. Who argues as stated by R. Chelbo in the name of Rav Huna that, if the holiday (Adar 14) coincides with Shabbat, all residents celebrate on the previous assembly day, Thursday? But, this makes little sense, for we already know that walled city residents would naturally read on Sunday, Adar 15. So, Rav Huna must have meant that any locale that must be changed because of a conflict with Shabbat should move its celebration back to Thursday. And, we learn that the "who" regarding Rav Huna's teaching is none other than R. Yehuda ha-Nasi.

Moving right along, why is it that we don't read the *Scroll* on Shabbat, as all Tannaim tell us? We touched on this on the previous *daf*, but reading or chanting the *Megilla* is a competence not achieved by everyone, there is the possibility that one, anxious to fulfill his obligation on the holiday, might take a copy of the text and carry it four paces in the public domain, a serious violation of a negative commandment on Shabbat. Rav Yosef offers an additional reason. We are obligated to give gifts to the poor on Purim, and poor people anticipate receiving them, but we can't be giving gifts on Shabbat, and that necessitates changing the date of the *Megilla* reading. Support for Rav Yosef's assertion that poor folk do indeed anticipate and dearly expect gifts next comes via a *baraita* that enjoins us to prepare such gifts to be distributed on Purim. And, this applies to whatever date the actual *Megilla* reading is assigned.

In a fashion not unlike that of Scheherazade, *lehavdl*, our *daf* end today with the word *aval* (but),

5a

whatever date the reading actually takes place, we learn here that the associated repast takes place "in its [correct] time" (*bizmanna*): Adar 14 (although some authorities differ on this point). Now, Rav avers that, if the *Megilla* is read at a time other than the "correct" one (Adar 14 for villages and unwalled cities, Adar 15 for walled cities), there must be a quorum of ten men present. Apparently, when read in its properly assigned time, any number (even by oneself) will do. Rav Assi disagrees—we always need ten men present, though if we can't assemble a full ten, then we must nonetheless read the *Scroll*. The key is to "publicize the miracle" of God's saving the Jewish people from destruction. The Gemara now interjects a statement from another rabbi in Rav's name which just might contradict this statement, and it concerns what is meant by "correct" or "proper" time for the reading of the *Scroll*: the day assigned by Scripture or the day, if necessary, to which the reading is reassigned when Purim happens to coincide with Shabbat. But, let's move on to the next Mishna.

The Mishna above covered large towns (bigger than villages but without walls) without specifying in more detailed fashion what it meant by "large." It now states that it must have ten idle men (*batlanin*) always ready and able to constitute a *minyan* (quorum of ten men) in the synagogue; fewer than ten such idlers constitutes a village. The former read the *Megilla* on Adar 14, the latter may have to move their reading to an earlier time slot. Now, we observed earlier that we are permitted, if circumstances require it, to shift the date of the *Megilla* reading back a day or more but never forward—so, for example, if Purim falls on Shabbat, we read it on Friday. The Mishna notes the possible oddity that, on many others prime events on the Jewish calendar, we can actually move the commemoration forward a day—e.g., if the fast of the Ninth of Av (commemorating the destruction of both the first and the second Temples in Jerusalem) falls on Shabbat, we observe the fast on Sunday. Furthermore, certain practices associated with the holiday may also be moved back to the day on which the *Megilla* is actually read. Finally, the Mishna cites R. Yehuda who clarifies what constitutes a village that is permitted to shift its reading back to an assembly day (Monday or Thursday); simply put, if people ordinarily do indeed go to the towns on assembly days, then it qualifies as such a village, but if not they must read the *Megilla* on Adar 14.

The Gemara's task, as always, is now to explain all this foregoing material. It starts with the ten "idlers," who our Tanna (and most commentators) see as men whose sole job is to sit in the synagogue as a constant *minyan*. Nothing more on this front at this time.

Now, turning to the more complicated issue of moving the *Megilla* reading back a day or more but never postponing it: Why? The same reason mentioned earlier, according to R. Abba in the name of Shmuel; namely, the oft-cited verse in *Esther* (9.27) states that "it shall not pass" (*lo yaavor*) which we have learned means that the reading cannot happen after the assigned date.

The Gemara next comes to the various events on the calendar which we are allowed to postpone, but not move back in time, if they fall on Shabbat. As for the Ninth of Av, commemorating as it does the destruction of both the Temples in Jerusalem, we must not advance remembrance of a catastrophe. It would be inappropriate to fulfill several of the other observances before the time we are obliged to do so, though wouldn't this apply to Purim as well? The one observance that requires a little more space is the *chagiga* offering, a peace offering brought on the first day of the holidays of Passover, Shavuot, and Sukkot; if that day coincided with Shabbat, the next day was the appropriate replacement. The Gemara asks specifically for the actual "time of the *chagiga*," as a *baraita* words it. Rav Oshaya offers an explanation, but even the Gemara basically agrees that this explanation gets us close to nowhere. Both Rava and Rav Ashi pipe up with further efforts to explain the *baraita*, but they get no closer to clarity except insofar as stating what we did at the outset (namely, the Mishna itself).

The Gemara now seems intrigued by the delay of a day regarding a theoretical coincidence of the Ninth of Av and Shabbat. R. Elazar reports a story in the name of R. Chanina to the effect that R. Yehuda ha-Nasi

5b

wanted to abolish the commemoration of the Ninth of Av. This point virtually jumps off the *daf*, as it seems utterly impossible; in fact, we learn from other sources that he sought to have it placed on a level with the other fast days during which the stringencies were not as harsh as they were for the Ninth of Av. The sages of the time didn't buy it, apparently. R. Abba bar Zavda fine tunes R. Elazar's claim by noting that R. Yehuda ha-Nasi's aim was not to abolish the commemoration altogether, but that the year he proposed this was one in which the Ninth of Av fell on Shabbat, when the fast would ordinarily be put off until the following day; and he just wanted to "abolish" the extra harsh stringencies for that year alone. R. Elazar then quotes the marvelously simple phrase from *Ecclesiastes* (4.9): "Two are better than one."

Before R. Yehuha ha-Nasi made his stark proposal, the Gemara also claims that he planted (a tree or just a plant) and then took a bath, both on a fast day. Gemara asks how he could possibly have done such a thing as planting, which qualifies as "work," something usually banned on holidays. Resolution (almost) too easy: R. Yehuda ha-Nasi lived in a city without walls, meaning he celebrated the holiday on Adar 14 and planted on Adar 15. "Almost" because the Gemara immediately points out that he was from Tiberias which definitely had walls in Joshua's day, meaning that he was designated to observe the holiday on Adar 15. What was he then doing planting on that day? The Gemara does a little fancy footwork here and switches things around: actually, he celebrated on Adar 15, precisely because Tiberias was a walled city back Joshua's era, and he thus did his planting on Adar 14. Just when you thought it had escaped a painted-into-the-corner situation, the Gemara notes that back in the day Chizkiya (Hezekiah) actually chanted the *Megilla* on both Adar 14 and 15, precisely because he wasn't sure about the status of walls in Joshua's time. Well, Chizkiya may have been uncertain, but R. Yehuda ha-Nasi wasn't, because he knew it had walls. The Gemara continues down this rabbit hole a bit further, but we shall leave it there.

Yet, the Gemara is not done with explaining how R. Yehuda ha-Nasi could plant anything on Purim. Rava's son Rabba says starkly that it was fine for him to do so, for what was forbidden on Purim was not planting (i.e., labor) but fasting and eulogizing. Jews never accepted a ban on work during Purim. His proof requires a little linguistic legerdemain, among friends. The term *yom tov* (generic word for holiday) is said to indicate a labor prohibition, but once Purim was a discreet holiday for the Jewish people, the only terms used in the *Scroll* are bans on fasts and eulogies. The absence of *yom tov* means there was no ban on labor.

Maybe three's a charm, for the Gemara wants to offer one more rationale for R. Yehuda ha-Nasi's behavior. Now, it is claimed that he did what he did *despite* the fact that the local practice was not to perform labor there on Purim, because he did it out of a sense of *simcha* or "joy." Planting for joy—such as building a home for one's son to be married in and live thereafter being one such example—can be justified on the holiday.

The Gemara isn't quite through with the decision (or lack of decision) made by Chizkiya regarding Tiberias in the days of Joshua. Apparently, there was a "fortress city" named Rakkat in Joshua's time, and it is now called Tiberias; "fortress" seems to imply walled. The Gemara clarifies that Chizkiya's doubt was regarding the fact that one of the putative "walls" was the side of the city facing the Kinneret (Sea of Galilee)—a "wall of water," if you will, and he didn't know if that counted as a genuine "wall." The Gemara doesn't like this explanation at all, and it cites a *baraita* which makes quite clear that "wall" is just that: an independent, standing, and circumscribing wall, not an ersatz, water wall. So, Tiberias is clearly out with respect to classification as a walled city. But, we learn at this late date, this is not what Chizkiya found confusing. It has to do with the definition of walled and unwalled cities right in the *Scroll of Esther*. The Gemara will surely return to this issue, but it now has other fish to fry.

Rav Assi reports that the *Scroll* was read on both Adar 14 and 15 in the city of Hutsal, because he did not know for certain if it had a surrounding wall in Joshua's time. The Gemara notes another account of Rav Assi's statement that, because Hutsal (in Babylonia) was part of the terrain of the tribe of Benjamin, the *Megilla* reading there took place on Adar 15.

It was noted moments ago that Tiberias used to be called Rakkat, a city mentioned in the text of *Joshua* along with two other places: Chammat and Kinneret. R. Yochanan begins an elucidation of the etymology of these toponyms.

6a

First of all, Chammat is Tiberias, but the obvious question is why it had that name then; answer: *cham* means hot, and Tiberias was famous for its hot springs. Rakkat, we are told, is none other than the city of Tzippori. What did it have that name? Answer: apparently, Tzippori is atop a mountain, namely higher than the terrain around it, like a river bank (*rakkat*) vis-à-vis the river. Kinneret was the city known as Ginosar. This etymology is a bit more far-fetched. The new toponym comes from *kinor* 'harp'; and that fruit from that city tastes as sweet as the sound from a harp. Rava must have winced hearing R. Yochanan's explanation for the first place name, as he offers a completely different understanding, one that ties Rakkat to Tiberias, not Tzippori. He cites two funerary practices that link the two names and that are (interestingly) attached to Babylonia. The Gemara adds a story regarding the passing of R. Zeira who was born in Babylonia but moved to the Land of Israel where he died; he was publicly eulogized with mention of Rakkat, but no mention is made of a city within the Land.

Rava now offers different toponomic connections for these cities. Chammat, he claims, is a place called Chamei Gerar; Rakkat is Tiberias; and Kinneret is Ginosar. The Gemara only asks about the second of these, and it responds that in Rakkat even "empty ones" (implying sinners; *rek* 'empty') there are as mitzvah-laden as the seeds of a pomegranate. This derivation is somewhat mystifying, as it says nothing about mitzvot; there are scriptural verses with words vaguely related to Rakkat that contain associations much more closely associated with good deeds, though they are not cited here.

R. Yirmeya says outright that city's true name is Rakkat, while Tiberias is just a descriptor. What does "Tiberias" (*Tiverya* in Hebrew) mean in this context? It's associated with the word *tibura* 'navel, center' implying the center of the Land of Israel. Rabba agrees about the Rakkat-Tiberias relationship, but he claims that the latter toponym comes from *tova riyya* 'fine appearance.'

Whereas R. Yochanan claimed Rakkat was another name for Tzippori, Zeira states next that Tzippori was known as Kitron. Tzippori acquired it name because it sits atop a mountain like a bird (*tzipor* in Hebrew). But, are the two places the same? Kitron allegedly was located in the part of the Land apportioned to the tribe of Zevulun. The Gemara here digresses to describe how it was that, when the Jewish people entered the Land, the tribe of Zevulun grumbled about its allocation. This material comes from *Judges*, and the story goes that Zevulun himself complained to God that he received poorer land than other tribes. Apparently feeling that He had to reply, God states that, because Zebulun had bodies of water on his land, he will have *chilazon*—those sea creatures from which a rare and distinctive blue dye (*techelet*) is taken and used for the ritual fringes (*tsitsit*) on garments—and his fellows from other tribes will come to him for them; apparently these creatures, whose identity is now unknown, crawl out of the water and up into the mountains. The verse in question (*Deuteronomy* 33.19) makes no specific mention of *chilazon*, but it does mention *sfunei* 'hidden things' which Rav Yosef identifies as *chilazon*. Zebulun still isn't placated and asks God about people stealing these creatures from him. God explains that, if *chilazon* are stolen, the *techelet* they attempt to make from it will not work.

The Gemara goes on to describe Tzippori which, as Zevulun saw it, was far better than the portion his tribe received. Reish Lakish testifies that he has seen it flowing with "milk and honey" (*chalav udevash*); he even offers measurements of the flow. Zevulun's land also had milk and honey but not like Tzippori, which Rabba bar bar Chana claims in the name of R. Yochanan is even bigger than what Reish Lakish claimed. So, then, if Tzippori was on the land allocated to the tribe of Zevulun, there would have been no possible reason to whine, and hence Zeira's equivalence of Tzippori and Kitron seems impossible. The Gemara suggests another possible explanation for his complaining, for suppose he had a vast expanse with milk and honey galore but he preferred fields and vineyards. Methinks God is being extremely patient.

The Gemara moves on to another place name. R. Abbahu cites *Zephaniah* (2.4) regarding Ekron which is said will be "uprooted" in future, based on the verb *ayin-kof-resh* which is also the base of the city's name. It is said to be the same as Caesaria which the Hasmoneans conquered from the Greeks. The Gemara segues here to R. Yose bar Chanina citing a verse from *Zechariah* (9.7) which makes no immediate sense whatsoever in this context. Eventually, Ekron is mentioned prophetically as a future site for Torah study. Still not fully clear, though the Gemara slowly but surely is drifting into stress on Caesaria. R. Yitzchak places it in tandem with Jerusalem: Rome or Greece vs. Israel. They mirror one another: one is in ascendant while the other is destroyed, but never are both ascendant or both destroyed. Rav Nachman bar Yitzchak cites a telling verse (*Genesis* 25.23) in this context; Rebecca learns that her twins will be harbingers of two great civilizations, Jacob for the Israelites and Esau for the Edomites (Romans).

More from R. Yitzchak on this topic follows. He recounts a passage in *Isaiah* (26.10) about how an evil man, even if given an opportunity to do right by according him a favor, will not behave righteously. The Gemara offers the example of an exchange between God and Isaac; Isaac suggests to God that his older son be shown some favor, although God warns him that Esau is no good and that the people who shall descend from him (the Romans) will destroy Jerusalem. A related lesson from R. Yitzchak, this time explaining a Psalm: Jacob tells God not to give in to Esau's wishes, because

6b

Gemamya (probably, Germanya), a region within Edom, will bring destruction everywhere they go.

Now that the Gemara had introduced teachings from R. Yitzchak concerned with the subject at hand, it digresses, as it often does, to lay out a few of his other (unrelated) thoughts. In virtually aphoristic form, he tells us that, if someone were to claim that he studied (Torah) hard but made no significant progress, don't count on it; and, by contrast, if he claims that he didn't study but did make progress, don't count on it either. Only if he claims to have worked hard and made meaningful progress are we to trust him. The Gemara limits this to studying Torah; in business it's all in the hands of heaven. Furthermore, even in the realm solely of Torah study, this refers not to comprehending what one is studying but only with respect to holding onto what one has learned to date.

Another from R. Yitzchak, this time citing *Psalms* (37.1): as for evil men who have achieved considerable fortune, don't mess with them, because you'll lose. They always win in court, defeat all enemies, and generally succeed. This is fairly disheartening news. Citing a teaching of R. Shimon ben Yochai, R. Yochanan disagrees; he cites a line from *Proverbs* (28.4), for Torah adherents do indeed mess with those evildoers who have abandoned it. The difference is a proper understanding of the psalm in question: it's not messing with the bad guys but attempting to compete with them that is self-defeating; similarly, we shouldn't pattern ourselves after their success or envy them. That's more like it. Also, the only one who can justifiably mess with bad guys is one who is completely righteous.

Last thoughts on this Mishna before moving on are introduced by Ulla. He states that "Italya of Yavan" (Greek Italy?) refers to Rome. He then gives its dimensions and describes something of what it looks like: over six square miles; 365 markets (one for each day of the year), the smallest of them for selling poultry (and its dimensions alone make it huge), and the king eats at a different one each day; 3000 bathhouses with hundreds of windows higher than the city walls for the steam to escape. On its four sides: the ocean, mountains, an iron barrier, and swampy land with gravel. Clearly, this is a wildly exaggerated depiction, but the implication is also clear: if such wonders are bestowed on a people always deemed evil in the Talmud, then just imagine what awaits the righteous.

Time, though, for a new Mishna. Because the solar calendar is 365 days, a second Adar has to be intercalated every so often to fill out the Jewish calendar. That opens the question as to when we read the *Megilla*: the first or second Adar? This all refers to the era before the fixing of a permanent calendar mentioned above. So, if the *Megilla* was read in I Adar and then the great Sanhedrin announced that there would be a second Adar, the *Megilla* was to be read a second time as well. This short Mishna concludes that, irrespective of what one did in I Adar, one must read the *Megilla* and distribute gifts to the poor in II Adar.

The Gemara begins by delineating what differentiates the requirements for the two Adars. There are four passages in the Torah read in synagogue in the weeks leading up to the holiday. They can be read in either of the two Adars. Three Tannaim don't buy this for a variety of reasons. Rav Pappa explains some of the complexity here. R. Eliezer son of R. Yose argues that the *Megilla* should be read in I Adar, and Rabban Shimon ben Gamliel claims that, if the four *parshas* (Torah portions to be read) were read in I Adar, they must still be read again in II Adar. After some more attempts to clarify, R. Chiyya bar Avin states (in the name of R. Yochanan) that the *halacha* accords with Rabban Shimon ben Gamliel who claimed (in the name of R. Yose) that, when a second Adar is intercalated, we are to read the *Megilla* and the four Torah *parshas* in II Adar.

R. Yochanan offers a little assistance in explaining all this as follows. R. Eliezer son of R. Yose supports his argument for celebrating Purim in I Adar from our old favorite verse from the *Scroll*: "in each and every year" we are to celebrate in Adar, the calendar month closest to (the previous month of) Shevat; Rabban Shimon ben Gamliel, who, as we have just seen, demands observance in II Adar, uses the very same verse and says we are to celebrate in the Adar closest to (the following month of) Nisan. There appears to be no particularly good reason for opting for either of these determinations. The Gemara tries to help here. R. Eliezer son of R. Yose would argue that we should never pass up an occasion to do a good deed, as soon as we know I Adar is coming, that's the appropriate time for the mitzvah. Why wait a month until II Adar? This is a preferable but not necessary practice, as it has no basis in scripture. Rabban Shimon ben Gamliel's retort is that, by celebrating the holiday closer to Nisan, we link Purim with Passover, two commemorations of redemption. R. Elazar even cites a supporting verse from the *Scroll* (9.29) which has the world "second" in it.

7a

Rabban Shimon ben Gamliel now argues that we need two sources to seal the deal. He cites this "second" taken from the *Megilla* and the earlier citation of "in each and every year." Independently, the explication could go either way, I Adar or II Adar, but together he argues that it can only mean II Adar. However, R. Eliezer son of R. Yose doesn't buy the interpretation of "second" as having anything to do with II Adar. He points out that it refers to a "second" letter that Esther and Mordechai were to send around the world proclaiming the observance of Purim, a teaching attributed to Rav Shmuel bar Yehuda. The Gemara uses this opportunity to cite a related point of this new rabbi, as he notes that Esther had an exchange with the wise men of old regarding a proclamation of Purim throughout the world about which the latter were reluctant but Esther insisted. Another exchange of this sort is now introduced by a group of four rabbis. Esther wanted the wise men to include the story of Purim in Scripture for all subsequent people to read. Again, they were reluctant, but ultimately they found an out enabling her request to go through.

The matter did not apparently end there, as some rabbis were not mollified allowing the *Megilla* into the canon. Citing Shmuel, Rav Yehuda claims that touching a scroll of Esther does not contaminate one's hands because it is not a canonized text. The backstory here is that each sage deemed touching a scroll of scripture renders one impure. But, did Shmuel actually balk at including the *Megilla* in the canon—was it not written under the influence of the divine spirit (*ruach hakodesh*)? In fact, he did think it was thus created. The Gemara clarifies: the *Megilla* was created for reading, not for writing and inclusion in the canon. This opens the floodgates: R. Meir claims touching a scroll of *Ecclesiastes* will not render one impure, though doing the same with *Song of Songs* remains undecided between the two great houses of Hillel and Shammai; R. Yose claims that touching *Song of Songs* will make one impure, meaning that he sees it as part of the canon, but the fate of contact with *Ecclesiastes* remains undecided; R. Shimon claims that *Ruth*, *Song of Songs*, and *Esther* all leave one's hands contaminated.

Never one to miss an opportunity, the Gemara takes a moment to digress and consider *Ecclesiastes* in this context. R. Shimon ben Menasya claims that touching a scroll of it will not contaminate one's hands, presumably meaning that he did not consider it a text of the canon. It was "merely" the wisdom of King Solomon, not a work inspired by the divine spirit. Rabbinic pushback points to a statement in *I Kings* (5.12) wherein Solomon is credited with no less than 3000 proverbs. This would indicate that *Ecclesiastes* is but a portion, a truly significant portion needless to say, of the kings' acute intelligence, and thus a divinely inspired text. The Gemara adds that in *Proverbs* (30.6), we are enjoined "not to add to his words," because Solomon selected which pieces of wisdom to include in *Ecclesiastes*, for those special pieces were, indeed, inspired by the divine spirit.

The Gemara now proceeds to offer several proofs by way of *baraitot* that the *Megilla* was divinely inspired. R. Eliezer cites the passage therein where the content of Haman's heart is noted—how would that have been possible except by the divine? R. Akiva cites the passage noting that everyone who saw Esther found her appealing—again, only the divine could have known this. R. Meir points to Mordechai's knowledge of the plot of Bigtan and Teresh to assassinate King Achashverosh, which could only have been divinely made known to him. And, R. Yose ben Durmaskit cites the passage in the text where it is noted that, when Jews in the Persian empire took action against their enemies, they did not seize any war booty, a fact that could not have been known for the entire empire unless the authors of the *Scroll* had received divine inspiration.

At a later date, Shmuel adds that he has an even better prooftext. The *Scroll* notes (9.27) that the court on high certainly sanctioned the reading of the *Megilla* on Purim; that would have necessitated divine sanctioning. Rava then goes Shmuel one further by not only agreeing that his proof was better than the other four rabbis but that those earlier ones each contained a flaw. So, starting with R. Eliezer, mightn't the authors of the *Megilla* have used logic to come to the conclusion about Haman's heart. R. Akiva's reasoning may be flawed in that each and every person who espied Esther may simply have seen in her someone of their own family, tribe, race, grouping. What about R. Meir? This one is especially interesting, for Bigtan and Teresh were from Tarsi; they spoke openly about their plotting in their Tarsi language, because they figured that Mordechai would not be able to understand. What they did not suspect (nor could have known) was that, because Mordechai was a member of the Sanhedrin, he knew all seventy languages (including Tarsi). Finally, R. Yose ben Durmaskit's proof, claims Rava, is inadequate; maybe envoys from faraway places in the empire reported that no booty was seized, even if it had been, so that Achashverosh would not become angry. Rava closes by noting the superiority of Shmuel's proof, and Ravina agrees and uses an interesting popular saying: "One sharp pepper is better than a basket full of melons (or pumpkins)."[1] On the surface, this is meant to tell us that one little pepper can literally spice up a whole meal, indeed far more than numerous melons; at one level remove, Shmuel was an Amora, a scholar from the period after the Mishna had been compiled, while the four proofs he incinerated were the work of four Tannaim, sages of an earlier and generally superior station.

The Gemara is not done, despite what one might sense to the contrary, proving the divine inspiration of the *Megilla*. Rav Yosef points to verse 9.28 which effectively prophecies the eternal celebration of Purim; and Rav Nachman bar Yitzchak cites the phrase in the same verse that offers the prediction that Purim will never be forgotten.

The Genera is now ready to move to another topic. When the discussion of I Adar vs. II Adar was raised, the questions concerned when the reading of the *Megilla* should take place—a topic now covered in considerable detail—and gifts to be given to the poor, the new topic. There are two kinds of gifts: *mishloach manot* are gifts to be sent to someone we deem worthy of their reception (two gift portions to one person); and *matanot laevyonim* are gifts solely for the poor (two gifts to two people). The Gemara now launches into a complex explication. R. Yehuda Nesia, grandson of R. Yehuda ha-Nasi, sent R. Oshaya the leg of a calf, the third born of the same mother, and a bottle of wine; R. Oshaaya wrote back that

7b

he'd fulfilled both sorts of gifts. There are various contradictory understandings of this line of text, but we'll leave it there.

More about gift-giving continues. Rabba sent two gifts to Mari bar Mar via Abaye: a basket of dates and a cup of fine flour made from roasted wheat; Abaye intimated that such gifts were beneath Rabba, his teacher, and he should have sent better items. On his way back Mari bar Mar had Abaye bring Rabba a basket of ginger and a cup of peppers. Again, Abaye felt compelled to comment that Rabba would note clearly that he had sent Mari sweet things and got bitter ones in return.

Rava relates another requirement of the holiday—that of drinking wine. Why? Because the three central elements of the miracle of Purim (Queen Vashti's disgrace, Esther's rising to become queen, and Haman's being put to death) all transpired in the midst of feasts of wine. But, not just a sip or two, for we are enjoined to drink enough wine (in the famous saying noted here) until you can't tell the difference between Haman and Mordechai. In other words, drunkenness is positively sanctioned. There was once an occasion when Rabba and R. Zeira were enjoying the Purim meal together and drank their fill. Apparently, more than their fill, as Rabba actually killed his colleague. He was so mortified that the next day he prayed for the revival of R. Zeira, and his prayer was answered (in the affirmative). When Rabba invited R. Zeira over the next year for the Purim meal, the latter (wisely?) demurred, noting that miracles don't always result from prayers for them.

Time for a new Mishna, a relatively short one, and from here until the end of this first chapter of the tractate, the content are unrelated to reading the *Scroll* and, for that matter, to any of the regulations surrounding Purim. What are they doing here, one might ask. Apparently, the style of their wording resembles previous Mishnas. So, then, this one only states that the only difference between Shabbat and holidays is the work related to preparation of food. That is generally prohibited on Shabbat but OK on holidays.

The Gemara immediately begins by noting what this allowable labor does *not* include. Direct food preparation is fine, but work preliminary to it is not; thus, slaughtering a chicken, for example, is allowed, but sharpening one's knife to that end is not. Shabbat and holidays are the same in this regard. R.

Yehuda, though, allows such preliminary work. The Tanna Kamma of the Mishna and R. Yehuda cite the same verse in *Exodus* (12.16) to support their positions, just different words in it. R. Yehuda stresses the term "for you" in the verse and sees it as meaning: for all the needs of persons preparing food; the Tanna Kamma argues that "for you" is meant to distinguish a Jew from idol-worshippers and animals. R. Yehuda similarly essays to debunk the Tanna Kamma's reasoning. No definitive answer is given to this difference of views.

On to a new Mishna, and this one states clearly that the only difference between Shabbat and Yom Kippur concerns how we deal with someone who violates the strictures associated with them. We are only dealing with punishment dealt out to those who desecrate the two days. A deliberate violation of Shabbat leads to the perpetrator being stoned to death; the same for Yom Kippur results in the perpetrator incurring *karet* (a punishment, usually of premature death, administered by God). R. Nechunya ben Hakkana rules that violation of monetary responsibility in conjunction with desecration of either Shabbat or Yom Kippur incurs no extra compensatory obligation.

If someone is condemned to lashes by the court and *karet*, the flogging is administered, but he is released from *karet* punishment. R. Chananya ben Gamliel explains, following a passage in *Deuteronomy* (25.3), that after one has received lashes, he is returned to equity with his "brother," meaning (presumably) other men. R. Yochanan jumps in here to say that R. Chananya ben Gamliel did not find his colleagues agreeing with this ruling. The actual wording of the Mishna is that violating Shabbat is punished by men, while violation of Yom Kippur is punished by *karet* (a divine punishment). If, however, one who is headed for *karet* incurs lashes and receives them, then human authority has replaced divine authority for this miscreant. Not a problem, as Rav Nachman moves to debunk this rejection of R. Chananya ben Gamliel's objection. This involves another *karet*-bearing sin involving outlawed sexual relations, in particular union between brother and sister.

8a

Another short Mishna followed by a short Gemara ensues. The wording here is a bit confusing, but it boils down to the claim that the only differences between someone who is banned from all advantage due to a vow and someone banned from any advantage related to food are the allowance to cross one's property and to use one's utensils that are not ordinarily used for food. The Gemara begins by trying to clarify—isn't the ban on all advantage and that on food-related benefit the same when it comes to the instruments used to make food? Does that explanation help? As for crossing another's property, the Gemara asks if that is such a big deal, given that most people wouldn't think twice about it. Rava avers that this teaching of R. Eliezer is embodied here, that crossing someone's property is gaining some advantage and it should be banned by virtue of the more general prohibition. This is a minority view, for the rabbis generally don't think of this as anything but ordinary human kindness.

The next Mishna and Gemara are only slightly longer. The only difference between vow offerings (*nedarim*) and gift offerings (*nedavot*) is that in the former case the person bringing it must provide for safekeeping, while in the latter case one is not responsible. So, the issue is liability. The Gemara starts by noting that both offerings must abide by the ruling "not to delay." The difference between these two types of offerings is still not entirely clear to the uninitiated. The Gemara offers an example from another tractate of the Mishna. For a vow offering, the vower states: "It is incumbent upon me" to bring this offering. For a gift offering, the gift-giver states: "This [animal to be sacrificed] is" an offering. Should the former vowed item die, get lost, or be stolen, the owner must bring a replacement; should the latter face such a fate, it is not the duty of the owner to replace the animal. The Gemara would now like to know where such legal authority comes from. It then takes recourse in *Leviticus* (1.4) where we find the word *alav* 'upon him' (in reference to a burnt offering) to distinguish the two types of offerings, as elucidated by R. Shimon. But, if you're still confused how this single word makes all the difference, so is the Gemara which asks how *alav* implies what R. Shimon claims. R. Yitzchak bar Avdimi lays all this doubt to rest by spelling out that "upon him" is clearly a reference to the onus of responsibility.

The next Mishna is also short, but this time we get a much more elaborate Gemara, if only because we are entering altogether dissimilar territory. The only difference between a *zav* (a man who has seminal, often gonorrheal, discharges) who experiences two such emissions (two the same day or one each on two consecutive days) and a *zav* who experiences three (on the same day or three consecutive days) concerns a particular type of offering (which the latter must bring but from which the former is exempt). Again, the Gemara begins by noting that both types of *zav* have the same requirement regarding the impurity that a *zav* transmits to a "couch and seat"—namely, no matter how many times he sits on it, they all become impure; both types of *zav* must go through seven clean days. How do we know this? Well, in a *baraita*, R. Simai points to verses in *Leviticus* (15.2–3) in which we are taught that two emissions are sufficient to render a *zav* impure, while three emissions necessitate a further burden of bringing an offering. There follows some give-and-take about the differences falling upon these two types of *zav*, but they lead nowhere in particular. Ultimately, we end up back where we started between a two-timer and a three-timer.

We move on to consider the seven clean days, meaning seven days free of discharges, required before the *zav* (either type) may cleanse himself by immersion in a *mikve* (ritual bath).

8b

We cross over briefly here to women and the emission of menstrual blood. Such a woman is dubbed a *zava*. Should she discharge blood on one or even two successive days during the period when she is not menstruating, she is dubbed a minor *zava*, and she need wait only one day free of discharge before she can immerse in a *mikve*. Comparison with a *zav* emitting on two days should, one might think, similarly necessitate one clean day, but the Torah states otherwise, explicitly affirming a seven-day clean period. This Gemara concludes with a question from Rav Pappa to Abaye about the intricacies and implications of not even a full word in the Torah but the prefix *mi* (from). Abaye explains in detail.

The next Mishna moves on to discuss a *metsora*, someone afflicted with a skin ailment known as *tsaraat* which is often translated as leprosy (but this is knowingly incorrect as even buildings can contract *tsaraat*). Should someone suspect *tsaraat*, he is looked over by a priest (*kohen*); if the latter suspects the possibility of the ailment, the *metsora* is quarantined for seven days and then assessed again. If at that point the priest adjudges this to be a positive case, he confirms his assessment. The Mishna claims that the only difference between a quarantined (suspect) case and a positive confirmation is that the latter must not cut his hair and must rend his garment. Similarly, the only difference between the return to purity (cure) from a quarantined or a positive case of *tsaraat* is that the latter must now shave his hair and carry out a procedure with a pair of birds not spelled out here (see *Leviticus* 14.4–7).

The Gemara begins by adding that both kinds of *metsora* are supposed to be banished from all three camps where the Israelites settled in the desert; in post-desert times, this would mean out of cities. Now, how do we know that the hair and rending obligations are only incumbent on a confirmed *metsora*? If the priest examines an apparent *metsora* and deems him not afflicted, he washes the clothes he is wearing (and himself) and is scot free of *tsaraat*, including the hair and garment-rending business *ab initio*. Rava doesn't buy it. The discussion now burrows down a rabbit hole, based largely on the tense of the verb regarding cleansing, and legions of post-antique commentators have toned in on this one. Rava is quite insistent that these requirements should also apply to the quarantined *metsora*.

Abaye jumps in at this point to probe Rava's thinking here. He follows Rava's reasoning and concludes on its basis that a quarantined *metsora* need not be banished from a walled city. But, this can't be so, because our

Mishna makes precisely the point that in this regard both types of *metsora* are identical. Rava is not ready to give up yet, as he offers a fairly odd rebuttal regarding the word "all" (*kol*) in *Leviticus* 13.46; since "all" is extraneous, in a common Talmudic practice, Rava seeks to homiletically explain that it implies "all" types of *metsora*, both quarantined and positive cases. Abaye makes mincemeat of this argument.

But, we now turn to a new Mishna, worded in the same way as the last few—"the only different between X and Y is Z"—but far from the realm of purity and skin ailments. This time: the only difference between the "books" (meaning Tanakh: Torah, Prophets, and Writings), on the one hand, and *tefillin* and *mezuzot*, on the other, is that the former may be written down in any language, but the latter are acceptable only in Ashurit script. "Ashurit" refers to the square-shaped Hebrew letters typical of the script used, even today, in writing such texts. Rabban Shimon ben Gamliel adds that the "books" could only be written in Greek (presumably meaning in translation).

Again the Gemara starts with an item that strengthens the point of the Mishna. We learn that scrolls of Tanakh, *tefillin*, and *mezuzot* all have to be sown together usually with flax; and if one touches such scrolls with bare hands they are rendered impure. The Gemara moves on to this curious point about the Tanakh being written in any language, but it raises a *baraita* that indicates a possible problem. That *baraita* indicates that the writing of a Hebrew text in Aramaic does not mean that it will convey impurity to the touch. Rava has a reply, effectively "no problem" (*lo kashya*), but it has to wait until the next *daf*.

9a

"Written" here refers to being written down, not initially composed. So, he explains that if transcribed in Ashurit script, it bears a holy status, but if rendered in more common Ivri script, the same text lacks such status. Abaye contests this explanation, as he reads the *baraita* to mean that not the script used to write down one of our texts in question, but the language (Hebrew and Aramaic) involved.

The Gemara tries another tack: it is the rabbis who deem a scriptural text holy even in languages other than Hebrew, but Rabban Shimon ben Gamliel rules that holiness devolves only on such texts in Hebrew. But, we should remember, it was this vary sage in the Mishna who deemed scripture in Greek to be legit. So, the *baraita* can't be Rabban Shimon's view. Another run at an explanation: "books" of scripture may be written in any language, but the *baraita* only concerns *tefillin* and *mezuzot* which have to be in Hebrew, because one of the texts included in them contains the word *vehayu* 'and they shall be,' implying they must endure as they are (no changes in language or script). Interestingly, the very line containing this word is from *Deuteronomy* (6.6) which, obviously, occurs in one of the "books," but no one mentions this. Still, the Gemara is not satisfied.

The next go at it states that the *baraita* in question is addressing the *Megilla*, and that text (the main topic of this tractate, we should not forget) has to be composed in Hebrew in Ashurit script. This sets it apart from other "books" which may be rendered in other languages. Yet, two of our ancient sages (Rav Pappa and Rav Nachman bar Yitzchak) immediately point to two places in the *Megilla* that have Aramaic words: *pitgam* for "decree" and *yekar* for "honor" (both 1.20), respectively. Once again, the Gemara tries to understand the Mishna: "books" of scripture may be written down in any language or script, Rabban Shimon ben Gamliel (referred to here as "our rabbis") allowed Greek as well. The Gemara wonders if Rabban Shimon's acceptance of Greek implies that the *baraita* meant to exclude it. This strikes me as unnecessary, but the Gemara as a rule leaves no stone unturned.

So, to clarify things, the Gemara now tries to reword the *baraita*. Rabban Shimon's permission for scripture in Greek must mean only for a scroll of Torah (not Prophets or Writings) for the following reason. And, this leads to an utterly fascinating tale involving King Ptolemy of Egypt. He assembled seventy-two elders of Israel and put them in seventy-two separate residences, without telling them why. (Kings can do such things.) He proceeded to visit each of them separately and request of each a Greek translation of the Torah. Stunningly, in this enormously famous story, they all independently came up with the exact same translation, with divine guidance. The worry was that divergent translations of key points could make Ptolemy suspicious that these scholars were up to something untoward. They began by rendering the first three words of *Genesis* in a different order: instead of *Bereishit bara Elohim*, they translated as if worded *Elohim bara bereishit* (God created in the beginning). The explanation for this shifting of terms was so that Ptolemy not construe the Greek term for "in the beginning" to be the name of some other deity—namely, you'd expect the name of God to appear first. Similarly, slightly later in this chapter of *Genesis* (1.26), where the original has God saying "Let us make man . . . ," our seventy-two sagely men changed it to the Greek for "I shall make man . . . " The former might be construed as there being more than a single deity. They made a similar change, from first person plural to first person singular, in *Genesis* 11.7 (the Tower of Babel story). The Gemara goes on to elaborate a fair number of the changes made to the text to overcome Ptolemy's eagle eye and not misconceive the holy text.

9b

As examples move from *Genesis* to *Exodus*, the translators strove to make Moses appear above the common run of men. The last of these borders on the amusing. Where *Leviticus* (11.6) names the rabbit as an unclean animal not to be eaten, our translators rendered it "the short-legged creature." Why? Because, as it turns out, Ptolemy's wife had a name, presumably Greek for "rabbit," that the king might have found offensive, if his wife's name were to appear in a list of non-kosher animals.

The Gemara to conclude this Mishna returns to Rabban Shimon ben Gamliel's teaching about the special place of the Greek translation of scriptural "books," and R. Abbahu (channeling R. Yochanan) claims that the *halacha* accords with Rabban Shimon's view. All of this may strike one as very odd, especially inasmuch as Greek has long since been off limits as the language for scripture. Today, and for a long time past, the Torah must be in Hebrew and transcribed in the Ashurit script. R. Yochanan comes up with a line from *Genesis* to justify this claim, but it is far from overwhelming, and (doing him a favor) R. Chiyya bar Abba offers a homiletical reading to enhance the thought.

But, we are ready for another Mishna, laid out in the similar linguistic format. The only difference between the anointed (with anointing oil) High Priest and the High Priest endowed via the donning of supplementary (eight) vestments is the bull that comes should there be any commandments violated. Similarly, the only differences between a presently serving High Priest and one who has had to step aside because he has acquired any impurity, or was intoxicated, or for some other reason are the bull presented by the High Priest on Yom Kippur and the one-tenth *ephah* (calculated to be a volume of some 43.2 eggs) of flour offered daily. Explanations to follow.

The Gemara begins by asserting that the Yom Kippur bull offering and one-tenth *ephah* are to be brought by the High Priest irrespective of anointment or extra vestments. But, then we learn that R. Meir, who can be a troublemaker, raised a *baraita* that the High Priest endowed only by virtue of extra vestments can also bring that bull. Our sages rebut him promptly. The Gemara wants to know how R. Meir can argue in this manner. Apparently, the relevant verse (*Leviticus* 4.3) speaks of "the" anointed High Priest, and the definite article is enough for R. Meir to include the High Priest with extra clothes. R. Meir also avers, in connection with the latter part of this Mishna, that if a High Priest must step aside and be temporarily replaced, when he returns to halachic fitness and regains his position, the replacement High Priest steps aside but must continue to behave as if he were in that exalted post—continue wearing the extra eight articles of vestment, etc. R. Yose has a whole other take, as he argues that when the original High Priest returns to duty, his temporary replacement not only does not continue behaving as if he is a High Priest *manqué*, but he no longer even continues as an ordinary priest. R. Yose then outlines the case of one R. Yosef ben Ulam of Tzippori who had precisely this experience. This seems rather harsh, but the R. Yose said they did this out of fear that a High Priest, after returning to center stage, might be angry (or jealous?) that there was another priest walking around in those eight extra vestments. But, perhaps even more interesting is that he cannot revert to an ordinary priest (who wears a mere four vestments). Why? An important Talmudic principle: *maalin bekodesh velo moridin* (we elevate but do not lower) in sacred matters. This principle applies in numerous instances, as we shall see later in this tractate.

So, it would appear as though the latter part of the Mishna accords with the view of R. Meir. Can it be that the former part reflects the view of the rabbis, despite a difference of opinions with R. Meir? Rav Chisda answers in the affirmative. Rav Yosef basically agrees, though he claims that the Mishna follows R. Yehuda ha-Nasi who himself puts these same two parts together in precisely this way.

Time for another Mishna, and this one concerns a *bama* (lit., a high place; pl. *bamot*) which usually means some sort of altar, though not the Altar either in the Tabernacle or the Temple. With several exceptions during pre-Temple days, it was prohibited to offer sacrifices on a *bama*. There are two types of *bama*: major or communal ones and minor or private ones. The only difference, as our Mishna states, in terms of offerings between the two types of *bama* is that the *pesach* or paschal offering may only be offered at the major one. The general principle here is that any voluntary (either vowed or donated) offering may be brought to a minor *bama*, but any compulsory offering may not (meaning it has to go to a major *bama*).

The Gemara here starts with a question, wondering if the only difference between the two kinds of *bamot* is the *pesach* offering. In fact, this very Mishna notes that compulsory offerings cannot be brought to a minor *bama*, which of course means they must come to a major one. So, the Gemara suggest that it means that any "like" *pesach* offerings come solely to a major *bama*, never to minor ones. That would mean all compulsory offerings that are fixed by date, and the Gemara wants to know whose ruling this would be. It then, as it so often does, responds to its own query by stating the culprit to be R. Shimon. A *baraita* is cited which states exactly that.

As our *daf* comes to a close, it introduces the first part of a Mishna which will finish up on the next *daf*. We now learn that the only difference between the laws concerning the Tabernacle when it stood at Shiloh and those at the temple in Jerusalem is that offerings of lesser sanctity (*kodashim kallim*) and second tithes (*maaser sheni*) were allowed to be consumed within sight of the Tabernacle, while once the Temple stood in Jerusalem, they had to be eaten within the city walls. Most-sacred offerings (*kodshei kodashim*) in both places had to be consumed "within the curtains" (meaning inside the courtyard of the Tabernacle in Shiloh or the walls of the Temple courtyard in Jerusalem). After the Tabernacle of Shiloh was destroyed,

10a

minor altars were permitted for the next fifty-seven years (in Nov and Givon) until the Temple was built in Jerusalem. After the Temple was destroyed, no such allowance was ever made.[2]

R. Yitzchak begins the Gemara by stating that he had heard of an allowance to bring offerings to Chonyo's temple. Chonyo was the son of the High Priest Shimon ha-Tzaddik; because of a series of circumstances described elsewhere in the Talmud,[3] he took refuge in Alexandria (Egypt), set up his own temple there, and offered sacrifices at it. R. Yitzchak argues that Chonyo's temple was not dedicated to idolatry; he also states clearly that when the Temple in Jerusalem was dedicated, it was for only as long as it stood, not for all future time, and thus following its destruction, other *bamot* were not prohibited. Truth be told, in Chonyo's time, the Temple *was* still standing. R. Yitzchak claims (citing *Deuteronomy* 12.9 which he uses to compare Shiloh with Jerusalem) that, just as after the destruction of the *bama* at Shiloh, it became allowed to establish *bamot*, so too should it be allowed following the Temple's demise. When word of this position got out, R. Yitzchak was confronted and asked if he had indeed actually articulated such a retrograde view. He denied it, meaning he retracted his position, but Rava makes plain that he heard the very words from R. Yitzchak who subsequently withdrew them when faced with a rebuttal from Rav Mari. And, what did Rav Mari say? He simply repeated the very words of this Mishna which point to this signal difference between the *bama* at Shiloh and the Temple in Jerusalem. He added the icing of a Mishna from *Zevachim* (112b) which not only states the same principle but says that such was the essence of the very verse R. Yitzchak cited. So, bottom line: no *bamot* after the demise of the Temple, and R. Yitzchak got the message and retracted his earlier stance.

That would seem to be a done deal, but one point seems not quite done. After the Temple was destroyed, did that terminate the holiness bestowed on it? The rabbis can never leave a stone unturned. The Gemara cites a lengthy Mishna, articulated by R. Eliezer, making the same point, only in greater detail, that while the Temple was standing, it acquired sanctity not solely for that time (while it stood) but for all time. This issue concerns the period following the destruction of the first Temple and the resanctification with the construction of the second Temple. Namely, was a resanctification necessary if the initial holiness survived the destruction of the first Temple? R. Yehoshua (in this other Mishna cited here) disagreed with R. Eliezer and argued that there was no need for Ezra to have resanctified the Temple when it was rebuilt. In a highly conciliatory gesture, Ravina suggests to Rav Ashi that, perhaps, both R. Eliezer and R. Yehoshua believed that the Temple's holiness never ceased; R. Eliezer merely heard what he stated above, and R. Yehoshua reported what he later heard. So, what's the issue in dispute? Apparently, nothing.

Not so fast. R. Yishmael son of R. Yose raises the question of resanctification by Ezra for walled cities other than Jerusalem, a process necessary for homeowners. If those other walled cities required it, how was it that Jerusalem appears to have been exempt? Thus, he concludes that the destruction of the first Temple must mean its holiness was terminated, and its sanctity did not last for all future time. Something is amiss.

10b

As we shall soon see, the very *baraita* being dissected notes that, if a city in the time of Joshua had walls, it required no sanctification anew. Again, if we can show that a city had walls in the days of Joshua, all the commandments that pertained then pertain now and for all future time. Sanctification then is sanctification now and into the future. So, the Gemara then asks on which side of the issue does R. Yishmael son of R. Yose ultimately come down, because he seems to be playing both sides. Actually, the Gemara saves the day for him, as it states that the two views were reported by others.

The fact that we are talking about walled cities again suggests that the text may be headed back to discussing Purim, Esther, the *Megilla*, and the like. And, indeed, that is the case, with no apparent segue. The Gemara cites the very first verse in the *Scroll of Esther*: "And it was [*vayehi*] in the days of Achashverish." It claims there is a tradition that whenever that word, *vayehi*, appears, we are headed into a distressing story. Exegetical commentary has it that *vayehi* is a combination of *vay* (pain) and *hi* (mourning). Examples ensue. This first line of the *Megilla* portends the appearance of Haman who tried to annihilate the Jewish people. Next: the first line of the book of *Ruth* has the same term and tells of a famine. Next: *Genesis* (6.1) tells of "and it was" regarding the population on Earth of humans, just as God adjudges great evil among men and plans their destruction. Next: the human plan to build a VERY tall skyscraper which God took to be of suspect, possibly idolatrous, motives and destroyed the Tower of Babel. Seven more examples follow, but I think the pattern should be clear.

These eleven examples should make a strong argument, but Gemara contests this conclusion, offering as an example a line from *Leviticus* 9.1

in which *vayehi* appears, regarding the eighth day of the dedication of the Tabernacle, and all was joy and happiness comparable to God's creation of the heavens and the earth from early in *Genesis*, which concludes "and it was evening and it was morning," day one. Actually, each of the passages there depicting God's creative work concludes with the quoted expression followed by the number of those first six days. Even that auspicious day of the Tabernacle's dedication was fraught with tragedy, as Nadav and Avihu, two of Aaron's sons, were killed at the time. The Gemara's defiant attitude stands firm, looking and finding other instances of decidedly positive events occurring after *vayehi*. First up: *I Kings 6.1* has our contested term introduce King Solomon's plans to build the Temple—certainly a joyous event. Similarly, Jacob's initial encounter with Rachel is introduced (*Genesis* 29.10) with this term. Summarizing, then, as noted above, each of the days of the week as God created parts of the universe conclude with the term (actually, twice each time, too).

This is powerful evidence, requiring Rav Ashi to step in and nuance the initial statement. Yes, he agrees, *vayehi* can present negative as well as positive times or events; when the text of scripture states *vayehi biyemei* (and it was in the days of), then it invariably leads to a distressing event. Five instances of the latter (all from Prophets and Writings) are adduced as proof: three already cited earlier and two new ones.

Seemingly out of the blue, the Gemara cites R. Levi, apparently because he was cited not so far back, who tells of a tradition he inherited that Amotz (Isaiah's father) and Amatzya (a king of Judah) were brothers. The Gemara asks the obvious question: So what? R. Shmuel bar Nachmani (in the name of R. Yonatan) explains that a modest bride, when in her father-in-law's home, will deserve great men—kings and prophets are mentioned—among her descendants. He gives the example of Tamar back in *Genesis*. And, indeed, King David was among those royal descendants, as Isaiah was among the prophetic ones—Isaiah was Amatzya's nephew, and Amatzya had to have been a descendant of Tamar (as were all Judean kings).

Another story from R. Levi: in the Holy of Holies of the first Temple, no space was taken up by the Ark. A *baraita* indicated the Ark's actual size as Moses built it (for the Tabernacle), and it describes the measurements as scripture indicates for the Ark, the wings of cherubim, and the like. Conclusion: it had to have been a miracle.

The Gemara moves now to a number of homilies as a means of introducing the *Megilla*. First up: R. Yonatan cites a passage from *Isaiah* (14.22) in which God promises an assortment of devastating horrors on Babylonia, and he provides (fairly allusive) exegeses on three of its words that indicate a relationship to the *Megilla*. Next up: R. Shmuel bar Nachmani cites a passage also from *Isaiah* (55.13), only this one is the effective flipside of R. Yonatan's, and this time we get a lengthy and much more adept exegesis of many of the terms and their homiletical meanings, a much more satisfying rendition overall. R. Yehoshua has his own introductory passage (*Deuteronomy* 28.63) to expound, a particularly harsh statement of God's willing desire to cause disaster among the evil people addressed. The Gemara pushes back that God does not as a rule gloat over those upon whom he brings destruction. Several sources follow to demonstrate this (decidedly anthropomorphic) notion that God does not enjoy the demise of evil types. R. Yochanan refers us to the passage in *Exodus* when Pharaoh's troops follow the escaping Jews into the Red Sea which then quickly closes up where it had parted and drowns the soldiers; His ministering angers were set to sing a song of praise, but God burst in to them and asks rhetorically: My creatures (all human beings, after all, even bad eggs) are drowning and you want to sing?! As R. Elazar concludes this discussion, basing himself on Hebrew grammar, it is not God Who delights in others' destruction; he makes others do the delighting. I'm not sure how different this really is.

Next we have R. Abba bar Kahana who introduces the *Megilla* with a citation from *Ecclesiastes* (2.26). The linkages between these two texts are thin, but that is often the nature of religious exegesis. I guess that's why they call it faith. We move on to Rabba bar Ofran who cites a passage from the prophet *Jeremiah* (49.38). The passage mentions a "king and princes," which our rabbi claims are elusive references, respectively, to Vashti (who in the *Megilla* is, of course, a queen, though not for terribly long, as well as the daughter of a king) and Haman and his sons—all wiped out, as the verse states.

As our *daf* comes to a close, Rav Dimi bar Yitzchak is about to offer up a verse to lead us into the *Megilla*.

11a

He cites a verse from *Ezra* (9.9) which speaks of God's having not having abandoned the Jewish people and having the kings of Persia show us mercy. The Gemara comments that this refers to the time of Haman who, unsuccessfully of course, wanted to kill us all. R. Chanina bar Pappa next offers a passage from *Psalms* (66.12) that mentions "fire" (a reference, allegedly) to King Nevuchadnetzar who famously had Chananya, Mishael, and Azarya thrown alive into a burning furnace and "water" (a reference, allegedly) to Pharaoh who ordered all Jewish male newborns thrown into the Nile; the verse from *Psalms* continues with praise for God's rescue of His people "into abundance," implying Haman's time (reference here to his failed effort to destroy the Jewish people and two central feasts recorded in the *Megilla*).

R. Yochanan launches his lecture with a citation from *Psalms* (98.3) which recalls that God's pledge of salvation for the Jewish people would reach to the ends of the world, a reference to the ultimate victory over the forces of evil.

Reish Lakish now offers his opening with a verse from *Proverbs* (28.15). It mentions "a roaring lion" (reference to Nevuchadnetzar) and "a growling bear" (reference to Achashverosh). Rav Yosef refers us to a *baraita* with some choice statements about Persians being just like bears (eating and drinking habits, hairy, fleshy, always on the move). Reish Lakish's citation also mentions "a wicked ruler" (reference to Haman, needless to say) and "a poor nation" (obviously, reference to the Jewish people, but the Gemara is not referring to ordinary un-wealthy but to "poor" in their observance of the mitzvot—as in they brought it on themselves?).

R. Elazar begins his commentary with a verse from *Ecclesiastes* (10.18) which makes little sense on the surface, and the Gemara switches immediately to homiletical explanation. The verse in question speaks of "laziness" which, we are told, means the Jews at the time of the Purim story had been ignoring Torah study; the result in *Ecclesiastes* is that the entire structure crumbles and presumably all goes to destruction. Again, it's their own fault. Rav Nachman bar Yitzchak has a more straightforward passage to lead into his lecture, taken from *Psalms* (124.1–2). It speaks directly to God's saving us when "a man rose up against us," obviously taken to refer to Haman.

Rava's chosen verse comes from *Proverbs* (29.2). The Gemara takes it aparts piece by piece: "When the righteous are exalted the people rejoice" (referring to Esther and Mordechai), for when (toward the end of the *Megilla*) Mordechai appears in his newly elevated royal garb, all Shushan came out to rejoice; and "when the wicked rule the people are in mourning" (referring, once again, to Haman), for when Haman sent out his proclamation for the eradication of the Jews, all Shushan was confused. Rav Matna begins with a verse from *Deuteronomy* (4.7) about a people so great all over the world, such that wherever they cry out to God, He comes to their rescue; the resonance here with Purim is too obvious for the Gemara to even comment. Rav Ashi also used a verse from the same chapter in *Deuteronomy* (4.34), this one referring to the salvation God performed when the Jewish people were suffering under Pharaoh which much resembles the later era under Haman.

The Gemara now segues subtly to begin an exegesis on a number of verses in the *Megilla*. The text begins, as we discussed earlier, with the word *vayehi* 'and it was [in the days of Achashverosh]' which Rav announces is a combination of *vay* (pain) and *hi* (mourning), as noted above. He goes on to cite *Deuteronomy* (28.68) which describes the calamitous retribution befalling the Jews for forsaking the *mitzvot*; again, this would seem to blame the Jews for their own suffering. Shmuel cites a passage from *Leviticus* (26.44) in which

God states that He will not break His covenant with the Jewish people. The Gemara sets offs on a roundabout exposition, but the meaning with respect to the Purim story seems fairly clear on the surface. The Gemara even cites a lengthy *baraita* which enumerates several such times in which God did indeed intercede to save the Jews, including the Haman and the Persians. Moving right along, R. Levi is the first to cite a passage from *Numbers* (33.55) concerning God's injunction to rid "the land" of all its inhabitants, for otherwise they will remain a constant annoyance (if not worse). Subtle reference to King Saul's failure to eradicate the Amalekites, including King Agag among whose descendants, putatively, was the much hated Haman. R. Chiyya prefaces his lecture with the Torah verse directly after that of R. Levi: If you (the Jews) don't rid the land of its inhabitants, I (God) may do to you what I'd planned for them; while that fate almost transpired, thankfully Haman was overthrown in the nick of time.

Now, back to our exegesis of the *Megilla*. Rav offers an exposition of the name "Achashverosh" as "achiv shel rosh" (lit., brother of [the] head). Who was the Persian king's "brother"? The Gemara says Nevuchadnetzar, but it can't mean that literally—maybe, "brothers" in the sense of similar character. Several scriptural phrases are proposed to make this connection, though they're rather slight. Shmuel, R. Yochanan, and R. Chanina offer some (almost playful) spins on the name Achashverosh to affirm his inherent evil, though their spins are on the Hebrew meaning of portions of his name (even reordering the letters therein) despite the fact that his was not a Hebrew name nor he Jewish.

Next we come to the phrase in the *Megilla*: "that is Achashverosh." Somehow, we are to understand this to mean that the Persian king was start-to-finish evil. How can such a reading be substantiated? I'm glad you asked, the Gemara effectively answers, as it now cites a series of phrases from scripture: "that is Esau" (*Genesis* 36.43); "that is Datan and Aviram" (*Numbers* 26.9); and "that is the King Achaz" (*II Chronicles* 28.22). At this point, the Gemara switches and introduces good guys, "start-to-finish": "that is Abraham" (*I Chronicles* 1.26) and "that is Aaron and Moses" (*Exodus* 6.27)—both righteous always; and "and David he was the youngest" (*I Samuel* 17.14) who was always humble.

Next words from the *Megilla*: "who ruled." Clearly, this refers to Achashverosh, but some say it bears a positive sense of the man, while other see it as derisive. It is, of course, impossible to say based solely on those two words "who ruled" (*hamolech*, actually only one word in Hebrew), but that never stops the Gemara from exposition. The *Megilla* goes on from here to explain the extent of this king's authority: "from Hodu to Cush." The perennial sparring partners, Rav and Shmuel, disagree on the meaning with one saying that Hodu stood at one end of the known world and Cush at the other—hence, Achashverosh held quite a kingdom; the other claimed that these two places, Hodu and Cush, were right next to one another, and as he ruled these two places, so he ruled his vast empire.

The next phrase from the *Megilla* reads tells us that he ruled 127 provinces, rather more than just Hodu and Cush. Rav Chisda reads this homiletically: so, the king started by ruling seven provinces, went on to rule twenty more, and ultimately ruled over 127 in all. Well, apparently, you can't use this kind of exegetical analysis unless you use it more generally, because the Gemara responds with *Exodus* 6.20 wherein we learn that Amram was 137 years of age. But, there's no similar explanation here, so Rav Chisda must have crossed a line. The Gemara, though, wants to salvage the *Megilla* verse, because it claims the "127 provinces" part is redundant; once it stated that Achashverosh ruled "from Hodu to Cush," the number is provinces is gravy, and that means that it is available for homiletical elucidation.

Picking up on the string of the Persian king's expansive empire, the Gemara now names three kings mentioned in scripture who "ruled the entire world": Achav, Achashverosh, and Nevuchadnetzar.

11b

Quickly, the Gemara suggests that maybe others also "ruled the entire world." How about King Solomon? Solomon was apparently left off the list because he didn't finish his reign, retiring before his time was complete. A number of other suggestions for why he is not considered a king of this sort are laid before the reader, but the Gemara concludes simply that Solomon's case was unique. Another contender would be Sancheriv (Sennacherib) whose conquests were admittedly considerable, though he never took Jerusalem. And, that's the stumbling block to his inclusion on the list. Well, then, what about King Darius (Daryavesh)? The Gemara cites a famous passage in the book of *Daniel* (6.26) in which Darius issues a royal proclamation to the entire world. Apparently, *Daniel* also mentions that Darius ruled 120 provinces, while we know that Achashverosh ruled over 127; that would leave seven to which he rule did not extend. One last try comes with King Cyrus (Koresh), and the book of *Ezra* (1.2) has Cyrus proclaiming his own rule over any and everywhere—what is left? The Gemara doesn't trust Cyrus because this appears to have been hyperbolic self-praise.

Back to exposition of the *Megilla* (1.2–3), where we seem to confront a contradiction. The verse in question begins with when King Achashverosh sat on his throne in Shushan which it takes to mean when he first did so, but it immediately thereafter states that he sponsored a feast in the third year of his reign. So, which was it, year one or year three, that the feast took place? Rava is the first to address this issue and claims it was the third year. This leads directly into a deep rabbit hole. Jeremiah (29.10) had earlier prophesied that Babylonia would rule over the Jewish people for seventy years, though he failed to indicate how one was to calculate those years. Nevuchadnetzar conquered Jerusalem and destroyed the first Temple; all these conquering kings knew of Jeremiah's prophesy, and seventy regular years later King Belshatzar (Belshazzar) was sitting on the Babylonian throne. He thus happily reached the conclusion the Jeremiah's words were null and void and had a huge celebratory feast, actually using some of the sacred vessels from the Temple.

But, Belshatzar's calculations were wrong. He claimed that his predecessor Nevuchadnetzar ruled for forty-five years, but there may be problems with this. The Gemara now launches a detailed accounting for the years of Nevuchadnetzar's reign. Actually, this part of the puzzle appears to hold up—he ruled for seven years before forcing King Yehoyachin from the throne in Jerusalem and then for a thirty-eight-year stretch afterward. That was followed by twenty-three years of rule by King Evil Merodach ("Evil" is part of his name, not an adjective) and the first two years of his (Belshatzar's) own rule which comes to a total of seventy. So, as he commenced his third year on the throne, he could "confidently" say that the promise of redemption of the Jews was much exaggerated. It was that very evening of his banquet that King Belshatzar was killed, and Darius the Mede came to the throne. This storyline comes from *Daniel*.

Learning from this, Achashverosh comes up with a different manner of calculating. He takes a closer look at Jeremiah's prophecy and decides that the seventy years doesn't start with the rise of Babylonia and Nevuchadnetzar's accession to the throne, but to the start of the Jewish exile caused by the conquest while Yehoyachin was on the Jewish throne, eight years into Nevuchadnetzar's reign. Calculating thusly, he comes to seventy years in the second year of his own reign: thirty-seven years of Nevuchadnetzar (following the defeat of Yehoyachin), twenty-three years of Evil Merodach, three for Belshatzar, five combined for Darius and Cyrus, and two years of his own.

So, convinced that those seventy years has transpired, Achashverosh followed his predecessor's example, exclaimed that Jewish redemption was finished, and hosted a celebratory banquet with sacred vessels from the Temple, presumably in conjunction with the third anniversary of his rise to the throne. Terrible thing to do, of course, and the Gemara tells us that Satan came and saw to it that the queen Vashti would be killed. What was wrong with Achashverosh's calculations, inasmuch as redemption would not occur for another eleven years? The starting point should not have been the exile of King Yehoyachin but the actual destruction of Jerusalem.

Now, to recalculate properly, we need to find eleven years and then the rebuilding of the Temple. That should coincide with the fourteenth year of Achashverosh's reign, but *Ezra* (4.24) has it that there were troubles in

Jerusalem which necessitated putting off the rebuilding until the second year of Darius's reign. The number don't work. Rava tells us that two of those seventy years were incorrectly calculated. Seventy is right, and it's not in Achashverosh's reign but in the second year of Darius, properly counted.

12a

The Gemara now cites a *baraita* that seems to indicate an earlier miscalculation: the total sum of the years that Israel was under the rule of Nevuchadnetzar and Evil Merodach comes to sixty-seven, not sixty-eight. The problem concerns the counting of partial years as full ones, and with Darius's first year on the throne, we come to a total of seventy. There is a further discrepancy, but this all ends with the extraordinary passage in *Ezra* (1.2) in which Cyrus commands the rebuilding of the Temple now that Jerusalem (and everywhere else) now falls under his hand.

Rav Nachman bar Rav Chisda strays momentarily to a verse from *Isaiah* (45.1) which suggests that Cyrus was God's "anointed one" (*mashiach*), and he asks if Cyrus was indeed the one. Actually, we are promptly told, the verse (properly read) means that God spoke to His anointed one (the real *mashiach*) *about* Cyrus; Rav Nachman clarifies that God had wanted Cyrus to start construction immediately as well as launching the ingathering of exiles, but Cyrus's proclamation was somewhat vaguer, allowing the exiled Jews to return to Jerusalem and rebuild their Temple. So, God was "complaining" (ignore the anthropomorphism here) about Cyrus to His "anointed one."

Back to the exposition of the *Megilla*, and we come to two verses from opposite ends of the text (1.3 and 10.2); in the former we find "nobles" of Persia and Media mentioned, while in the latter we read "kings." Why the difference here? Rava "explains" that Persia and Media had an arrangement whereby they alternated which group sat on the throne and which served as governors in the provinces. Thus, the two verses reflect different times.

More from the *Megilla*, and this one concerns the passage (1.4) describing Achashverosh's "glorious" (*kevod*) kingdom (and his "magnificent" [*tiferet*] greatness, as the verse continues but is not directly cited in our text). R. Yose bar Chanina notes that both terms resonate with a verse in *Exodus* (28.2) describing the garb donned by the High Priest, and he concludes that the Persian king himself donned the same garb stolen from the Temple.

The next verse from the *Megilla* (1.5) introduces the king's feast for everyone living in his capital of Shushan, but only after inviting those outside the capital. Rav and Shmuel have a difference of opinion about the king's plans for feasting, though (as is often the case) we don't know who held which view. One said this shows how wise Achashverosh was; he could easily placate Shushan residents whenever he wished, so inviting those outside first was a good call. The other thought this demonstrates his foolhardiness; had he first invited locals to a feast, they would have stood by him in the event of a rebellion led by those outside the capital. Apparently, Achashverosh had had problems with certain provincial administrators whom he had had to put down, and this renders the Rav-Shmuel dispute rather more meaningful.

More on the same verse from the *Megilla* follows with an interchange between R. Shimon ben Yochai and his disciples. This assumes that, as the verse states, everyone in Shushan (including presumably the Jews) were present at Achashverosh's feast. The students ask their teacher why the Jews at that time warranted eradication by Haman, which of course is averted in the eleventh hour. R. Shimon ben Yochai throws the question back, and they reply because they attended and enjoyed evil Achashverosh's feast. He goes on to aver that, logically only the Shushanite Jews would have been in attendance, so why were all the Jews, even those elsewhere in the world, to be murdered by Haman's diktat? This time his students don't know, and he explains that those Jews elsewhere had bowed down to an image or idol of Nevuchadnetzar. This is a bit confusing, as the Tanakh depicts the refusal of Chananya, Mishael, and Azarya to bow down before this image, but it thus assumes that all the other Jews did just that presumably out of fear. R. Shimon has some sharp disciples, for they now ask him why the prostrating Jews in Nevuchadnetzar's time were given a pass; aha, says their teacher, their bowing down was only a superficial gesture, never meant to be done out of genuine principle. How convenient! And, God responded in kind by merely scaring them into contrition. In any event, annihilation was never in the cards.

The next *Megilla* verse (1.6) requires the Gemara's explanation. In describing the king's palace, it mentions "*chur, karpas*, and blue," all hangings on the walls. So, what is *chur*? Rav claims that they were tapestries with numerous holes, where the word *chur* is related to the word *charei* (holes); Shmuel, of course, disagrees and says *chur* refers to white wool, where *chur* is related to *chivar* (Aramaic for white). On to *karpas* which R. Yose bar Chanina claims means cushions made with velvet, dissecting the word *karpas* in half: *kar* (cushion) and *pas* (velvet or fine wool).

This same verse in the *Megilla* goes on to describe the couches, some gold and some silver, on which Achashverosh's guests sat for the feast. R. Yehuda claims that seating arrangements called for certain guests to deserve silver and more elite guests to deserve gold couches. R. Nechemya responds that distinguishing places in this manner would have incited jealousy, so it was much more likely that all the couches were silver with golden legs.

The Gemara lingers on this verse because of a number of terms that require explication and the apparently requisite disputation. Let us sample a few. The *Megilla* speaks of *dar* and *socharet*. Rav explains the former term to refer to the numerous rows (*dar* means "row") of magnificent inlaid stones in the palace floors; Shmuel claims that *dara* refers to a highly valued stone to be found in cities by the sea. A third voice, that of R. Yishmael, suggests that the king used this opportunity to announce a diminution of the sales tax for local merchants, presumably on the basis of the similarity of *dror* (freedom) to *dar*. All three of these sages also implied resonances with *socharet*, but this should suffice.

The following verse in the *Megilla* (1.7) begins with a question about the cups used for drinks at the feast; the suggestion raised by Rava is that a voice rang out from heaven that the king should beware, because Belshatzar used goblets seized from the Temple and it spelled his destruction; Achashverosh would be very wise not to repeat that error. If the king heard the voice on high, he must have ignored it. The *Megilla* (same verse) goes on to tell us that the guests were given lots of wine. Rav inserts that this can't mean a lot of wine but must mean aged wine, older than the guests themselves. The following verse inserts something interesting, even odd. It states that drinking at the feast was conducted "according to the law" (*chadat*). What law would that be, you might ask. R. Chanan (in the name of R. Meir) claims that it was the Torah's law that one should eat more than drink, and the king (referred to here, as elsewhere) as that "evil" one. One commentator suggests why Achashverosh would have bothered with this dictum, and he concludes that the king did not want to make Belshatzar's mistake—namely, he understood his predecessor's error not in using sanctified Temple vessels for a profane feast but in using them to excess (inebriation).

The next verse of the *Megilla* (1.8) implicitly states that everyone at the party was given wine from his own home province, wine that he would know how to consume in moderation. It continues with something about each guest's enjoyment, and R. Elazar relates this to Mordechai and Haman who served at the feast, though the connection is a little difficult to make.

The *Megilla* (1.9) moves on to (then-) Queen Vashti who was simultaneously throwing a banquet for women. Where? The Gemara suggests that the text should have specified that her women's feast was being held in the women's quarters, but Rava disagrees, as he see both the king and queen were fully prepared to engage in acts of immorality, each having sex with others in attendance; thus, she held her feast close by her husband's to facilitate this. Hence, the popular saying of the day: he with big pumpkins and his wife

12b

with small pumpkins, implying that both of them were readying themselves for the same thing.

With considerable attention devoted to the *Megilla*, we are still only up to verse ten of the first chapter. It tells us that Achashverosh was feeling happy with his wine on the seventh day of his big bash. As if a very early take on the old joke about a filial Jewish son and his mother,[4] the Gemara asks if this means he wasn't joyous on the previous six days. Rava has an explanation (which also has a modern ring to it): the seventh day for Jews is Shabbat, and on the day Jews eat and drink and discuss Torah, but idolaters like the king eat and drink and move right into licentious affairs. That's why the king was so happy. Some of them would say Medean women are more beautiful than Persian women, while others would reverse the comparison; Achashverosh broke the tie, saying that the most beautiful women are Chaldean, like his wife Vashti. The king offers to call her for inspection, and his guests jump at the opportunity but only if she appears in her birthday suit, the essence of her beauty all the more apparent. The Gemara suggests that this fate awaited Vashti, because she had compelled Jewish girls in the past to dance in the nude for guests.

Well, as the story continues, Vashti refuses her lord's demand (*Megilla* 1.12). This poses a problem, for acting in an indecent manner can't be the reason for her refusal; the Gemara just (on *daf* 12a) noted that the royal couple was planning some sort of depraved behavior. R. Yose bar Chanina has an answer and a fairly ludicrous one at that: she had only just broken out in *tsaraat* and didn't want the rash to be visible to the assembled guests. If this one seems strange, a *baraita* offers an explanation even more *outré*: just then the angel Gabriel appeared and had her grow a tail. Whatever her reason, the king was extremely angry. Anger is surely understood, but why very angry? Rava think he knows: Vashti sent the king a message in which she calls her spouse a "stable boy" of her father, Belshatzar, a man who could drink Achashverosh under the table without becoming an idiot and thus making such embarrassing demands of her. The king's anger grew to white heat.

In the next verse of the *Megilla* (1.13), the king turns to his wise men to speak, but before the text can identify these guys, the Gemara intercedes with a who question: Who would those guys have been? Answer: the Jewish sages, which seems quite strange. The text immediately describes them as those "who knew the times." This odd phrase means that we are talking about men who knew how to intercalate months into the calendar, and apparently only the Jewish sages could do that. The Gemara, not the *Megilla*, says here that the king asked them what he should do about Vashti. The sages are in a bind; if they suggest capital punishment for defying a king's orders, then when he sobers up the next day and realizes what has happened, he will blame them for advising him to execute his beautiful wife; if they suggest he just release her, that would be impossible because she publicly humiliated the king. It's clear they couldn't possibly care less about Vashti, who is frequently referred to as "wicked," just like her husband. So, they cop out and tell the king that they have lost their ability to make judgments ever since the Temple was destroyed and they were forced into exile; they suggest he go and ask Ammon and Moab who haven't experienced exile and dispersion.

Satisfied with this resolution, the *Megilla*'s exegesis rolls on (1.14). So, the king turns to others of his men closest as hand, all of whom have odd names requiring creative exposition. R. Levi starts by claiming that the entire verse refers to sacrificial offerings. "Karshena" is explained as lambs (*karim*) of the first-year (*shana*); "Shetar" is explained as two turtledoves (*shete torin*); "Admata" is explained as a mound or altar of earth (*adama*); and "Tarshish" is explained as one of the priest's vestments (lit., a beryl); "Meres" refers to stirring of the blood of sacrifices to be applied on the Altar; "Marsena" is understood as a mixture of stirred (*meirsu*) *mincha* offering, but we're beginning to stretch the boundaries of language here; finally, "Memuchan" derives from a prepared (*muchan*) table. In each of these instances, the ministering angels ask God, according to the Gemara, if the goyim ever did any of these things for Him.

This last fellow, Memuchan, then speaks, but the Gemara is not interested in what he has to say; it identifies him as Haman, citing a *baraita*. How does the *baraita* know such things? It now interprets the *muchan* embedded in the name as "destined" of "fated" for punishment, either applying it to the Jewish people or his own ultimate execution. Rav Kahana spots something interesting here. Memuchan is mentioned last in the list of Achashverosh's aides, meaning he was the least key player, but he jumps to the front of the group to reply to the king. He offers the king his advice, and the latter then sends a royal edict throughout the realm to the effect that every man should rule over his own house (*Megilla* 1.22). This strikes absolutely no one as particularly interesting or insightful. If edicts are this silly, the Gemara reasons in an effort to understand the popular mind, then why bother even paying them heed. The second one, though—and here is the connection with Haman—calls for the destruction of Jews.

The *Megilla* turns now (2.3–4) to the advice given the king for the selection of a new consort: assemble all the lovely maidens of the realm and choose one. Rav reminds us of a similar event in the life of David, and who wouldn't want to be related to the royal family this way? Achashverosh, though, wanted all the daughters of the realm brought to the palace so he could pick one, but only after he had violated them all seriatim. This being the case, every father hid his daughter.

The *Megilla* (2.5) now introduces Mordechai, of the tribe of Benjamin. The text of the *Megilla*, skipped over here in the Gemara, provides three names to trace Mordechai back to his father, grandfather, and great-grandfather. Why all three, and if they're necessary, why not all the names back to

Benjamin himself? They have got to be there for a reason, and now we get brief expositions on these names, all indicative of Mordechai's character. So, "son of Yair" implied that he "enlightened" (*yair* from *heir* 'brightened') the eyes of the Jewish people through his prayers; "son of Shimi" implied that Mordechai's prayers were "heard" (*shimi* from *shama* 'heard, heeded'); and "son of Kish" implied "knocked" (*kish* from *hikish* 'knocked') on the gates of mercy and was permitted entrance.

The same verse identifies Mordechai as *Yehudi* ('from the tribe of Judah') and later *Yemini* ('from the tribe of Benjamin'). Which is it? The simple answer, of course, is that the former doesn't strictly mean of the tribe of Judah but any "Jew." But, the Gemara rarely settles for simple answers. Rabba bar bar Chana (in the name of R. Yehoshua ben Levi) explains. In actuality, Mordechai's father was a Benjaminite, and his mother was from the tribe of Judah. While unusual to introduce someone by their maternal tribal affiliation, special honors are accorded Mordechai here, honors over which both tribes contended.

13a

R. Yochanan has an interesting take on Mordechai's origins. Yes, he was definitely a Benjaminite, he avers, but why then do we call him a Judahite? Answer: Anyone refusing to bow down to idols may be so considered, because Chananya, Mishael, and Azarya who heroically refused were of that tribe. R. Shimon ben Pazi does a spin on the personal names in *I Chronicles* (4.18) to substantiate this reading about rejecting idolatry. On the surface it is just a listing of names, patronyms, and the like, but R. Shimon ben Pazi reads much into those specific names mentioned. "Yehudia" should really be understand as Bitya (Pharaoh's daughter), the young woman who saved Moses from drowning and who would herself come to repudiate idol worship; a Torah verse (*Exodus* 2.5) describes her going to the river to bathe, which R. Yochanan reports was her immersion as a convert and to cleanse herself of her family's whole infatuation with idols. Not only that, we learn that, by adopting baby Moses, she effectively had assumed the place of his mother and could so claim. Next up, the name "Yered" which the Gemara states is actually Moses himself. How so? The Hebrew word *yered* implies *yarad* 'it came down'—some take this to refer to the *manna* that fell from Heaven to feed the Jews while they were in the wilderness (due to Moses' accrued merit); others claim it refers to the fact that Moses "brought down" the Torah from Mt. Sinai. The other names in the verse—Gedor, Chever, Socho, Yekutiel, and Zanoach—are all also connected homiletically to Moses.

R. Shimon ben Pazi notes that the verse referred three times to "the father of" and not every time to Moses, so it can't be taken literally. Once released from literalness, the Gemara claims that Moses was, indeed, the "father in Torah," "father in wisdom," and "father in prophecy." He concludes this bit with a spin on the name, Mered, the Jewish husband of Bitya, but it is really quite far-fetched.

Let's get back to the *Megilla* (2.6). The *Scroll* mentions Mordechai's exile from Jerusalem, which Rava informs us was accomplished solely at his own initiative. The next verse (2.7) introduces the heroine of this story: Mordechai raised Hadassa, the original Hebrew name of the woman who would become Esther. The Gemara's fixation on names is fascinating, and it immediately asks which of those names was her real one. R. Meir cites a *baraita* to the effect that it was in fact Esther; she bore the name Hadassa because she was righteous, and righteous people are referred to a myrtle (*hadas*), citing a verse from *Zechariah* (1.8). R. Yehuda turns this around, stating that her real name was Hadassa; she acquired the name Esther to hide her Jewish roots (H. *hester* 'concealment'), as verse 2.20 makes clear. Wait, there's more. R. Nechemya agrees that Hadassa was her original name and that "Esther" was a name used by many because she was extraordinarily beautiful—her name resembles (sort of) the Aramaic word for "moon." Ben Azzai, who always has something worth listening to, pipes up with this point: she was a young woman of average height, just like a myrtle. That would mean that her real name was Esther, and Hadassa was a popular epithet. Final explication: R. Yehoshua ben Korcha says her original name was Esther, but she had a greenish hue to her facial skin, like a myrtle, and she had something of kindness in her appearance. Green?

Let's move on the next piece of this same verse of the *Megilla* where it states that Esther had no living parents, which was why Mordechai raised her, but then it says that her parents died. Isn't that redundant, asks the Gemara. Rav Acha explains that her father passed away when her mother conceived her, and the latter died in childbirth. Thus, neither ever really lived long enough to be called a true parent. At the end of verse 2.7, the *Megilla* tells us that Mordechai adopted her as his own daughter. R. Meir apparently suggests that Mordechai actually married Esther, but this detail never surfaced at the time. This strange reading reads *bat* 'daughter' as *bayit* 'home'—frequently in scripture a man's "home" is depicted as his wife. The Gemara cites a passage in *II Samuel* (12.2) to substantiate the exegetical legitimacy of reading *bat* as *bayit*, though I'm not sure what this does for our understanding of the Purim story.

Moving right along, the *Megilla* (2.9) recounts the famous part of the story in which Achashverosh finds Esther pleasing and turns her over to a group of seven maids to start treating her like a proper queen. Why seven? Rava explains that Esther needed this number to keep count of when Shabbat arrived, using one each day. The end of the verse states that the king offered

Esther some sort of special kindness, but it doesn't say what that was. Rav makes the odd suggestion that he provided her with kosher food, which makes little sense inasmuch as she was concealing her Jewish identity. Au contraire, Shmuel states that she was given pig bacon of some sort, while R. Yochanan says they were seeds of some sort. The text actually says nothing about food of any sort, so this remains on the level of wild speculation.

This was still a trial period that the king was checking out candidates who would pretty themselves up for his "inspection." This process of beautification involved six months of using "oil of myrrh" (2.12). The Gemara wants to know that that is. R. Chiyya bar Abba says it's another name for balsam, but Rav Huna claims that it is the oil of olives still in the first third of their growth period, meaning still unripe. R. Yehuda says that this kind of olive oil is called *anpakinon*, a word clearly of Greek origin. The Gemara asks why they would smear this oil on their bodies and replies that it is a kind of depilatory that allows one's skin to shine.

The procedure (described in *Megilla* 2.14) was that each evening a young woman would come to the king and return the next morning; that was it, unless the king wanted her again. At least it happened at night, the Gemara notes, as sexual relations during the daytime was considered immoral. When it was Esther's turn, everyone loved her (2.15). R. Elazar suggests that Esther appeared in the eyes of everyone who observed her as if she was a member of their ethnic nation. Esther was brought (2.16) to the king's palace in the tenth month of the year, Tevet, a colder month of the year which, according to the Gemara, is a month when the body seeks greater contact and desires from another's body, all of which played into Esther's hands, so God must have set up the timing that way.

We all know where this is going. Achashverosh preferred Esther to all the other women (*Megilla* 2.17). The verse actually mentions both women and virgins with whom the king cohabited, meaning he had his pick. Esther is now to become his queen, and the kings puts on a big feast (2.18). Meanwhile, following Mordechai's instructions, she still had revealed to no one that she was a Jewess. Achashverosh performs a number of good deeds in her name, hoping to elicit her ethnic origins (according to the Gemara), but she demurs.

The *Megilla* (2.19) then announces that all the maidens were called together once again. Mordechai was also at the palace. That's all the verse actually says, but the Gemara has the king approach Mordechai and ask him how to extract this information about ethnic origins from Esther. Now, Mordechai was the very person who had told her the word was mum on that topic, but Achashverosh didn't know that detail. Bottom line: she kept her background concealed (2.20).

At this point the Gemara leaps down a rabbit hole of digression with R. Elazar citing a verse from *Job* (36.7)

13b

that notes how God never forgets the good deeds performed by righteous men and women. It will be interesting to see what connection this has to the Purim story. Way back when, Rachel was a highly modest woman, so much so that God deemed Saul among her descendants. Saul, too, turned out to be a modest person, and therefore God deemed Esther among his descendants—there is, actually, no evidence for the latter lineage. The Gemara now presents the whole Rachel-Leah story in such a way that Rachel does, indeed, appear to be modest and nowhere nearly as deceitful as Jacob: she and Jacob have a plan to outsmart Laban, but Rachel realizes that it will embarrass her big sister, so she can't go through with it, and Jacob ends up with two related wives. Evidence of Saul's modesty? The Gemara relates with much greater brevity a moment from *I Samuel* (10.16) in which Saul, having just been anointed king, has an opportunity to gloat before his uncle and chooses not to do so. There is a limit to this modesty business. The verse from *Job* we are addressing ends with God's remembrance of righteousness becoming a perpetual phenomenon continuing for generations, but should arrogance ever replace modesty, game over, as the very next verse (6.8) in *Job* states clearly, it will end very poorly for them, very.

We left the *Megilla* at 2.20, where Esther does as Mordechai asks, which seemed clearly to point to concealing her identity. R. Yirmeya, however, relates this to her presenting traces of her menstrual blood to Jewish sages to conclude if she was truly in the midst of her period, based on their reading of the color of the blood. No good Jewish woman would engage in cohabitation during the days of her period. Esther would then leave Achashverosh's bedchamber, clean herself up, and go to Mordechai, whom the rabbis seem to think was her true husband. The problem here is that, once a woman has had relations outside of marriage, she is forbidden to her husband, and this the rabbis get around by claiming that she was forced, against her will, into the king's bed to begin with.

The next *Megilla* verse (2.21) relates another famous piece of the Purim story. Mordechai was again situated at the palace gate, when he overhears a plot being discussed by Bigtan and Teresh, two angry men planning regicide. R. Chiyya bar Abba (in the name of R. Yochanan) claims that God set it up this way and sees a much earlier resonance of it: just as He made a lord become angry with two angry underlings so that a righteous man should appear on the scene, enter Joseph and the two chamberlains in prison. The chamberlains ended up in prison presumably because Pharaoh was angry at them, but with the result that Joseph emerges and rises to greatness in Egypt. A bit roundabout, but this is like Mordechai's route to prominence in Shushan: God makes two guys angry with their lord so that a righteous man may do the right thing, deemed a "miracle" (*nes*) here. The next verse (2.22) recounts that Mordechai learned of this plot, told Esther, and she told the king what Mordechai had reported to her.

As far as the plans of Bigtan and Teresh are concerned, this is as much as the *Megilla* tells us. They are executed (2.23) in a suitably gruesome manner, and that is all; the whole story is an elaborate mechanism to get Mordechai to become a favorite of the court. But, the rabbis can never let it drop that easily. R. Yochanan relates a story to one we confronted in R. Meir's exposition on *daf* 7a. Namely, the two hapless servants were speaking in the Tarsi language within earshot of Mordechai and complaining that, ever since Esther entered the palace, they hadn't known a moment's rest; the assumption is that the king was continually have relations with Esther and calling on them to remedy his thirst. So, they plan to put poison in his drinking bowl. What they didn't know was that Mordechai's service back in the Temple included time in the Chamber of Hewn Stone, and he was thus conversant with all seventy languages (meaning all the languages of the world). They thought he couldn't understand them, but (unluckily for them) he knew Tarsi. The rabbis even lay out what the two men said to each other for their plan; in short, it is revealed and they pay the final price.

That scene ends the second chapter of the *Megilla*, and verse 3.1 begins "after these things." It goes on to report that the king raised Haman through the ranks to the peak of the officialdom, but the Gemara is stuck on what those "things" refers to and how they are related to Haman's rise. Rava states that God first comes up with a solution and then presents the problem; this is a little confusing but let's leave it there.

The Gemara now jumps over several verses to *Megilla* 3.6, which strikes this reader as somewhat odd, as those elided are incredibly pertinent to the story. They tell of Mordechai's refusal to bow down to Haman, Mordechai's Jewishness is revealed, and Haman's rage knows no end. But, as verse 3.6 notes, the evil Haman decides not to eliminate Mordechai but to use this opportunity to eliminate all the Jews in Achashverosh's entire kingdom. The verse speaks of "the people of Mordechai" and then "all the Jews." Some translations see the later term as appositive to the former, but Rava suggests that the former was separate and referred to the rabbis, meaning that Haman first wanted to have Mordechai executed, then the rabbis, and then all the Jews.

So, the *Megilla* (3.7) next tells of Haman's insidious plan to draw lots (the meaning of "Purim," by the way) to decide the day on which he would do away with the Jews. First, it falls on the month of Adar, and a *baraita* tells of Haman's glee at this eventuality because it would coincide with Moses' death, and that would be a highly unfavorable month for the Jewish people.

How he would have known the month in which Moses died or why he didn't simply choose Adar (was he even planning this according to the Jewish calendar?) are not related. The precise dating of Moses's death is not confirmed in *Deuteronomy*, but the rabbis figure it to be Adar 7. However, we do know that Moses died exactly on his 120th birthday, which means Adar wasn't such a bad month for the Jews after all.

The following verse (3.8) tells of Haman tattling to the king not solely about Mordechai but about the whole Jewish people who are spread throughout his realm, who have laws different from those of the king, and who ignore the king's laws—conclusion: there's no good reason for the king to brook such insolence. Rava comments that, if Haman excelled in one thing, it was as a defamer. When he proceeds to suggest to the king, in Rava's exposition, that the Jews be extirpated, Achashverosh balks out of fear of the Jewish God who destroyed earlier rulers who tried to achieve the very thing that Haman was now suggesting. In a much more dubious development of this dialogue, Haman supposedly claims to the king that God won't protect them, because the Jews have not been following their own commandments, but again the king balks because, he claims, their rabbis surely have been following the *mitzvot*. But, Haman won't rest until he gets royal authority to carry out his massacre, so he tells the king that the Jews behave as a unity, "one nation," and the rabbis are just like the other miscreant Jews. Second-guessing the king, Haman says, in this fictitious dialogue, that perhaps the king thinks that some of the Jews far and wide in the kingdom may provide some value to him, but it is not true, for they are like a mule—an interesting, if crass, simile—in that they are barren, nothing good or useful can come from them.

Haman then, allegedly, goes into detail. When he said that they had their own distinctive laws, he meant that they refuse to eat Persian food or marry Persian women, and they won't allow their women to marry Persian men. The verse also mentions that they ignore the king's laws, by which Haman meant that they don't work as hard as they should, taking off every seventh day for their Sabbath and the eight days of Passover. When he urges the king not to brook the Jews' disrespect before the realm, we learn that Haman meant that they mock the throne. Example: should a fly plop into a glass of their wine, they scoop it out and continue drinking, but if the king so much as touches the glass, it becomes prohibited to a Jew.

After all this, Haman suggests (*Megilla* 3.9) that the king issue an edict for their annihilation, and he (Haman) will personally place 10,000 talents of silver in the royal treasury to finance the operation. Reish Lakish has a homiletical reading of this verse, but it is too bizarre for me to elaborate here.

So, skipping verse 3.10 to which we shall return shortly, *Megilla* 3.11 recounts that Achashverosh gives Haman carte blanche to proceed with his sinister plan and provides the money himself. R. Abba

14a

sees an allegory at work here. It's like two men—one has an empty ditch, the other a pile of earth—who will each pay so that the ditch can be filled up (the former) and the earth removed (the latter). They then bump into one another, realize that their solution is right there before their eyes, and it costs neither of them. Similar, Haman and Achashverosh both want the Jews destroyed, and when Haman was willing to front the job with his own money, the king was pleased enough that they agreed on the goal and even to forego the money. One can only wonder why the king was so worried earlier about Haman's plan and sought to forestall it.

Now, what about verse 3.10 which we skipped? It merely states that the king took his signet ring off and handed to the Haman, and although we have only started *daf* 14, the ensuing digression will almost completely fill the entire *daf*, which also may explain why the Gemara dealt with 3.11 first. So, what is this ring all about? R. Abba bar Kahana leads the way. By having the king slip the signet ring off his finger and hand it to Haman, this meant he was acceding to Haman's wish to issue an edict for the destruction of the Jews. But, that's obvious and not the point R. Abba bar Kahana is making. He claims the act of removing the ring was more significant that all the words of the Jewish people's forty-eight prophets and seven prophetesses. Why? For all the efforts of these prophesying men and women, they never were able to get the Jews to hew to the path of righteousness, whereas the impact of that slipping the ring off his royal finger led the Jews onto that pathway.

A *baraita* now begins the explanation of this intriguing statement. Whereas all these prophets and prophetesses never exceeded or diminished in any way the laws laid out in the Torah, there is one exception: they in fact inaugurated the annual reading of the *Megilla* itself. Why did they do this? R. Chiyya bar Avin argues (in the name of R. Yehoshua ben Korcha) that, surely, if the Jews sang their famous Song of the Sea, praising God for enabling them to escape slavery and Pharaoh's drowning soldiers, then the reading of the *Megilla* as celebration for God's saving them from destruction at the hands of Achashverosh and Haman seems equally appropriate. So, then, we should recite the *Hallel* prayer, a song of praise for God after deliverance from imminent disaster, to accompany Purim. Yet, we do not recite *Hallel*, because it commemorates a miracle that transpired beyond the Land of Israel's borders. This can't be right, because we just compared the events in Purim with the escape from Egyptian slavery, and the latter obviously took place outside those same borders. And, we do recite *Hallel* at the advent of Passover. A *baraita* explains that, before the Jews entered the Land, songs of praise for God, as in *Hallel*, were acceptable wherever they took place, but once they entered the Land, Israel was the only acceptable site for praising

God's miracles in song. The experiences recorded in the *Megilla*, of course, took place much later, and for that reason reciting *Hallel* when observing the holiday of Purim is inappropriate.

Rav Nachman can't leave well enough alone. He claims that the recitation each year of the *Scroll of Esther* is the functional equivalent of the recitation of *Hallel*. Rava raises a problem with this. At the beginning of *Hallel*, one finds the verse "Give praise, servants of God," completely appropriate when the Jews had escaped from Egypt and were no longer under Pharaoh's thumb, but after being saved from Haman's evil plans, weren't they still servants, so to speak, of Achashverosh? Would that not rule out recitation of *Hallel* on Purim? The Gemara avers that, after exile from the Land—meaning after the destruction of the Temple and Jerusalem—the Jews reverted to their pre-Land station, and thus *Hallel*'s recitation was allowed.

A *baraita* above spoke of forty-eight prophets, but the Gemara points to a verse right at the beginning of *I Samuel* (1.1) which mentions a man (Elkana) from a place called Ramataim-Tsofim. There is no mention of any numbers here, but numerology (*gematria*) administered to the lexical element *mataim* (from Ramataim) is similar to the Hebrew word for 200, just as the first letter, "r" (*resh* in Hebrew), in *gematria* is also understood as 200. Were there actually 200 prophets in Elkana's time? Seems a bit steep. The Gemara concedes that there were undoubtedly more than forty-eight, the only ones recorded for posterity being those who prophesied about repenting in the Jews' future behavior or teachings to that effect. Various subsequent efforts have been made to identify who the forty-eight were, but the jury is out on a couple of them.

What about the seven prophetesses? Who were they? The Gemara now names them: Sarah, Miriam, Deborah, Hannah, Avigail, Chulda, and Esther (maybe suggesting where we're going with this lengthy digression), but it can never resist the temptation of a discursive analysis of names. We start with Sarah, our first foremother and wife of Abraham, and the Gemara cites a verse from the middle of *Genesis* (11.29) and then quotes R. Yitzchak to the effect that one of the persons named in the Torah verse, Yiska, was actually Sarah. But, why was she so called? The Gemara connects "Yiska" to the verb meaning to see or look, and later in *Genesis* God tells Abraham to "heed her voice" in all matters, meaning that she has powers to "see." As R. Yitzchak goes on to state, her vision was inspired by the holy spirit.

On to Miriam as prophetess, and here the Torah states explicitly (*Exodus* 15.20) that she was a prophetess. The same verse notes that she was Aaron's sister, but it doesn't make unambiguous that she was also Moses' sister. Rav explains that she was prophesying before Moses' birth, indeed prophesying that their mother would bear a son who would "save Israel." The story in the Gemara gets a little rocky at this point, but ultimately, of course, Miriam was right.

How do we know that Deborah was a prophetess? She is revealed as a prophetess, literally, in *Judges* (4.4) in a verse that states she was the "wife of Lapidot." A homily on this name follows: she was said to make wicks for the menorah in the Tabernacle, alluded to by Hebrew *lapid* 'torch' (plural, *lapidot*). More on Deborah: she would do her prophesying while seated beneath a palm tree. Why? One rabbi explains that the branches of palm trees are far from the ground, and thus when one is under them it was clear that she was not with someone other than a parent, child, or spouse, which would have been indecent.

Hannah is not explicitly named in Scripture as a prophetess, so it has to be derived. In *I Samuel* (2.1) she is quoted as stating that "her horn is exalted in God." Sure enough, it was a horn of oil that was used to anoint David and Solomon as kings, and their reigns were quite long. However, when a "flask of oil" was used for Saul and Yehu, their reigns were not nearly as long. The Gemara continues with an exposition of Hannah's prayer at this point in Scripture; not directly related to her endowment of prophecy, these passages reveal the beauty of her insight into the numinous realm.

Avigail is also not specifically named as a prophetess. Her story occupies this rabbit hole and burrows further into another. We are still in *I Samuel* (25) and a nighttime meeting between her and David.

14b

She confronts him about condemning her husband Naval to death for failure to supply David with food, apparently impugning his honor. David apparently believed that, although not yet king, he had been anointed and that his honor had been assailed. Avigail responded that Saul still sat on the royal throne and David's renown was a thing of the future. Thus, Naval's action may not have been nice, but it did not constitute a rebellion. I don't know how many times this happens in Scripture, but David (a man) is convinced by Avigail (a woman) that her logic is superior to his. And, he praises her for preventing him from executing someone unfairly. This apparently is evidence enough to qualify her for prophetess status, but the Gemara reads another point which may indicate prophetic character into *I Samuel* (25.31–32) in which she cautions David not to let "this be a stumbling block to him." Whatever it may originally have been referring to in Scripture, the Gemara suggests that it was an intimation that Avigail could foresee the problem David, quite the womanizer, would have down the road with Bathsheba. Our text makes numerous references to David's solicitation of Avigail's favors which she fends off one by one.

Chulda is next, and she is identified in scripture (*II Kings* 22.14) as a prophetess to whom men went for advice. She was doing her work at a place and time where Jeremiah was also at work, and he preceded her by several years. How could she get away with that, for wasn't this some sort of insult to him? In fact, there was no proscription on her doing this, as both Hannah and Miriam did the same (at the time, respectively, of the prophets Eli and Aaron). Someone in Rav's academy reports Rav teaching that Chulda and Jeremiah were related, so he had no complaints to report. The passage in *II Kings* mentioned above tells of men sent by King Yoshiya to Chulda, and the Gemara wonders if that was appropriate. It responds promptly that the academy of R. Sheila claimed he did that because women are more compassionate than men. The idea is not that women would clean up a fateful future by replacing bad with good, but that they would deliver such a message with more mercy and pray ever so hard to alleviate a possibly disastrous prophecy.

R. Yochanan offers a different explanation for the king's action in this instance. He sent his men to Chulda, because Jeremiah was out of town at the time on a mission to reclaim the ten tribes. There is some back and forth here, but we are led to believe that Jeremiah succeeded. How do we know that Yoshiya did come to rule over the ten tribes? The Gemara relates a story from *II Kings* (23.17) about Yoshiya going to Beth-el to destroy idols; Beth-el was within the kingdom of Israel, and the assumption then is that he came to rule over it, which was where the ten tribes were located. There is also some talk about a prophecy of Judah, but it is fairly murky.

Finally, we come to Esther. The *Megilla* (5.1) tells us that Esther "clothed herself in royalty" rather than in royal garments. The extrapolation is that "royalty" implies divine inspiration, and thereby we get a connection to her capacity as a prophetess. This exposition is by far the Gemara's shortest of the seven women in this category.

Having laid out all seven women and why they qualified for prophetess status, the Gemara has Rav Nachman propose a series of teachings about them. Haughtiness is not an attractive quality in a woman, he claims. (Is it attractive in a man?) He points to two of the seven just discussed and (again) zooms in on their names which he deems repugnant: Deborah (whose name means "bee" in Hebrew) and Chulda (whose name means "weasel"), both of whom acted haughtily toward men. They should have been aware, we suppose, that born with such degrading names, they needed to act with greater humility. Cherchez les parents!

Actually, that's just what Rav Nachman does, as he digs into Chulda's lineage. He claims she descended from Joshua, but this is far from established fact. R. Eina the Elder presents a different, more elaborate line of descent that has Chulda a descendant of Rachav. Rav Nachman addresses R. Eina

54   Chapter 1

directly—and not in a particularly attractive way, at least not on the surface—
and suggests that they put their two points together: Rachav was a proselyte
who Joshua married. Rachav is thought to have been a member of one of the
Canaanite nations, folks Joshua was expressly prohibited from marrying. The
answer, found elsewhere in the Talmud (*Yevamot* 76a), is that she was not
Canaanite but happened to be living in Canaan at that time. A new question
now presents itself, as it was thought that Joshua had no offspring. Simple
answer: no sons, indeed, but he did have daughters.

15a

When discussing R. Eina's take on the lineage of Chulda on the previous
daf, we skipped over a brief digression about eight prophets. Four of them—
Jeremiah, Chanamel, Baruch, and Seraya—the Gemara now notes, we accept
because they're explicitly so identified in Scripture, but the other four, who
just happen to be their fathers (respectively)—Chilkiya, Shallum, Neriya,
and Machseya—are not, which means the Gemara will now explain how we
know all this.

Ulla begins by introducing an analytic principle. Most prophets are so well
known that Scripture names them without a following patronym. If it does
so in the form of prophet X, son of Y, then Y is also a prophet; if there is no
patronym, the father was not a prophet. Not directly related but important,
Ulla adds that, if a prophet is named followed by his city's name, then that
city is where he is from; if there is no such toponym, then the prophet is from
Jerusalem. A *baraita* adds that if Scripture selects for praise prophet X, son of
Y, then we are to assume that both were righteous men; similarly, by contrast,
should Scripture select for harsh criticism X, son of Y, then we are to assume
that both are awful.

Continuing in this genealogical bent, Rav Nachman at this point states
what on the surface appears to be an absurdity: the prophet Malachi was
Mordechai from our story. He explains that he was given the prophet's
name because he was number two to the king, apparently based on the word
"Malachi" which is close the Hebrew *malach* 'angel.' The Gemara then cites
a *baraita* to the effect that a number of prophets issued their prophecies at the
same time—regarding the reconstruction of the Temple—and Malachi and
Mordechai are recorded separately. This is what the Gemara calls a *teyuvta*
or a definitive refutation.

R. Yehoshua ben Korcha now pipes up with an almost equally ludicrous
genealogy: Malachi and Ezra are one and the same, and this time it is just
as swiftly shot down. Malachi was that prophet's one and only name. Rav
Nachman, who seems to have forgotten or abandoned his earlier identification, now avers that the Malachi-Ezra formula is probably right. He notes

that Malachi excoriated Jews who had married gentiles, and it was Ezra who compelled them to divorce their non-Jewish wives. The Gemara does not contest this supposition—at least, not yet.

The Gemara returns to have more to say about Rachav. She is listed in a *baraita* cited here with Sarah, Avigail, and Esther as a woman of extraordinary beauty. The Gemara suggests R. Yehoshua ben Korcha (see *daf* 13a), who reported a greenish facial hue to Esther, would replace her with Vashti. The rabbis of old actually state that a simple declaration of the name Rachav aroused sexual yearning—no explanation follows with even a homily or *gematria*. Similarly, Yael had the same impact with her voice, Avigail by recalling her memory, and Michal simply by her physical beauty. If all this isn't enough to remember that the Talmud was written by and for men, R. Yitzchak makes the extraordinary statement that, by just calling out the name Rachav twice in succession, one would have a seminal discharge. Rav Nachman admits no such response to her name, and R. Yitzchak clarifies that he is referring to men who have "known" her.

The Gemara now return to exegesis on the *Megilla*, though it has skipped over several chapters. We turn to Mordechai crying out (4.1–2), as the Gemara asks what he actually said while crying out. Though mentioned nowhere in the text, Rav claims that he yelled something to the effect that Haman was now more powerful than Achashverosh, because Haman's plans for the annihilation of the Jews was something beyond which the king had actually dreamt. Shmuel claims that Mordechai euphemistically made the point that the earthly king appears to have triumphed over the one on high.

Moving right along, verse 4.4 notes that, when Esther is informed of what has become of Mordechai, she was very, very upset. Rav explains her agony as meaning that she menstruated; R. Yirmeya claims that it is a reference to the loosening of her bowels. The next verse (4.5) states: "Then Esther summoned Hatach." Rav then claims that this Hatach is none other than Daniel. We know from other mentioning of him in the *Megilla*, that Hatach was Jewish, and no other Jews were known among the king's high officials. Even Shmuel gets into the fun by actually agreeing with Rav and offering homiletical identification of the name Hatach. In the same verse, Esther sends Hatach out to Mordechai to find out what was going on that made her relative behave as if in mourning.

We come now to a well-known part of the *Megilla* in which Mordechai informs Hatach of Haman's plans for the Jews and asking him to have Esther implore the king to prevent this from happening. Esther famously demurs because she knows that appearing before the royal personage without an invitation can be punished with execution; she asks Hatach to relay this to Mordechai. The *Megilla* (4.12) then states that "they" (not "he" or Hatach) relayed this information to Mordechai. The Gemara reads this as meaning

Esther sent her response via others, and the lesson to be derived is that one ought not rush back on such an assignment with bad news—odd, particularly if the news is really bad (as in this case).

Esther, of course, has a heroic change of heart, and (verse 4.16) she sends a message to Mordechai that he should get all the Jews of Shushan together, have tham all fast for seventy-two hours, as she and her entourage shall also do, and then she will proceed to risk her life and approach the king, contrary to the law of the land. Not unexpectedly, the rabbis have a sexual reading of this passage, relating it to her change from unwilling to willing partner with the king in marital relations. There appears to be no good reason for this explication. The next line from Esther is utterly famous: If as a consequence of approaching the king on my own, I die, then I die. The Gemara reads this as her stating to Mordechai that, if she now willingly submits to the king, she can never return to Mordechai as his wife (which has itself been read into the text, of course).

So, in the next verse (4.17), we learn that Mordechai "passed" and did as Esther told him to, which means, according to Rav, that the general fast began on the first day of Passover. Needless to say, there is no mention whatsoever of Passover in the text. Shmuel merely reads "passed" as his having traversed a river from the palace to Shushan proper to gather the Jews together and relay Esther instructions. The *Megilla* (5.1), as noted on *daf* 14b, next tells of Esther proceeding to "clothe herself in royalty," a teaching of R. Elazar in R. Chanina's name.

As it often does, the Gemara now takes this opportunity to cite a long list of teachings that R. Elazar reports in the name of R. Chanina, some more closely related to the story of Purim than others (to be noted below with an asterisk). We start with: Blessings offered by otherwise insignificant persons should never be ignored. Cases in point are David and Daniel. Daniel's blessing (*Daniel* 6.17) came from none other than Darius; Darius was hardly insignificant, though he wasn't Jewish. By contrast, a curse issued by someone otherwise insignificant should also not be ignored. Avimelech (*Genesis* 20.16) had negative words for Sarah about losing her sight, a fate delivered to her son Isaac (*Genesis* 27.1) years later when he began to go blind in his old age.

The third teaching contrasts ordinary men and women with God, using a strange example. People first put their pots on the stove and then add water, but God does it in reverse and gets the water in the right spot and puts the pot around it. The prooftext (*Jeremiah* 10.13) basically explains that God puts the waters together in the sky and then surrounds them with clouds. In addition to being highly anthropomorphic, most of us can probably come up with stronger proofs of the difference between ordinary people and the Deity.

Neither of the last two instructive lessons had anything to do with the *Megilla*, but the next one does. Relaying a report in the name of the person initiating it affords redemption to the entire world. The proof is Esther's telling King Achashverosh (*Megilla* 2.22) of the plot against him by Bigtan and Teresh. As a result, Mordechai was promoted and put into a position to later sniff out Haman's far worse plot.

Next teaching: the death of a righteous person is only for his own time, for his spirit continues. No verse is recorded to substantiate the point, but the Gemara states simply that, if someone owned and then lost a pearl, that pearl (somewhere) remains a pearl. Only the owner has lost it.

Another: Haman (*Megilla* 5.13) observed Mordechai seated by the palace gate and said that it meant nothing to him. What could he have meant, other than the obvious point that he had no use for Mordechai, Esther, and the Jews? Rav Chisda has a midrashic explanation: Mordechai had (much earlier) been rich and Haman

15b

poor. The midrash actually has Haman having sold himself into slavery for Mordechai who purchased him "for loaves of bread."

The next teaching draws on a citation from *Isaiah* (28.5) and claims that in future all the righteous will have God as a "crown of beauty and a diadem of glory" on their heads. Explication involves linguistic similarities between the "will" of God and the word used here for "beauty," and between those who "await" God's "glory." The tail end of this verse states that such a fate is only for the "remnant of His people," meaning not for everyone but only those who are relatively insignificant, humble folks. The Gemara goes on at this point (drawing on *Isaiah* 28.6) to list scriptural references to those it deems "righteous" in this sense: someone who offers correct judgments often by suppressing an evil inclination; someone strong enough to suppress the same evil inclination and not sin; someone who engages in Torah study and debate; and men who study Torah from dawn until dusk.

Isaiah goes on (28.7) to discuss how alcohol can cloud, even disfigure, one capacity to judge properly. The Gemara turns this into a question raised by the "attribute of justice" before God and God's response. The "attribute of justice" asks the Lord why Jews are rewarded for their proper judgments while other people are not. God replies (as it were) simply that the Jewish people study Torah, while other nations do not. This rendition, then, turns a discussion of the negative impact of wine on judgment to that of making correct judgments leading directly to Gehinnom (Hell). Textual support ensues, but enough said on this front.

Back to the *Megilla*, though we have to go back to a verse (5.1) addressed earlier, albeit a different part of that verse. The part we confront now mentions that Esther was standing in the inner court of the palace. R. Levi notes that to get there, Esther had to walk through the chamber of idols, and it was at that point that the Shechina (divine presence) left her. She had just clothed herself in "royalty," which we learned above meant divine inspiration as she was on her way to speak to the king, but that would now have ceased. Although none of this is in the *Megilla*, she immediately calls out to God in one of the best known *Psalms* (22.2): "My God, my God, why hast thou forsaken me?" Esther offers several explanations as to why she has been stripped of a modicum of divinity, but the Gemara doesn't develop any of them further.

Instead, we return to exposition of the *Megilla* (5.2). This is the verse in which the king looked at Esther and she won favor in his eyes; and he then "extended the golden scepter" to her. R. Yochanan comments that three angels, each assigned a separate task, accompanied Esther at this precarious moment: one raised her neck (she had been exhausted and famished from three days of fasting), one spread grace over her, and one made sure the extended scepter reached her. The idea, apparently, is that she was so famished and tired that she could barely walk. How far, asks the Gemara, did the third angel have to extend the scepter. R. Yirmeya avers that it went from its ordinary length of two paces to twelve; some even state that it reached sixteen, while yet others say twenty-four; a *baraita* says sixty—quite a scepter! Lest one find this barely credible, the Gemara offers two other cases in which an item was stretched well beyond the ordinary in apparent performance of a miracle. The first was when Pharaoh's daughter, whom we encountered earlier, reached out to gather in baby Moses from the Nile. The second instance comes from a bizarre story of a giant, Og king of Bashan, who was intent on destroying the Jews, but a miracle enlarged his teeth so he couldn't move. The Gemara ends this digression with a word from R. Eliezer relayed by Rabba bar Ofran: the scepter extended to 200 paces.

Back to the *Megilla* (combining verses 5.3 and 5.6) in which Achashverosh asks Esther what she may want, and he twice tells her that he is ready to give her as much as half of his entire kingdom. The Gemara notes that "half" here is related to "divided" in half, and what lies at the point dividing the kingdom in half would be the site of the Temple, deemed the center of the world. This indicates that the king would never allow its rebuilding, because that would encourage the Jews to rebel against him.

One of the verses (5.4) between the two mentioned immediately above has Esther asking her king to make sure that Haman comes to the banquet that she is throwing that day. The Gemara asks why she wanted to be sure that he would be there. On the surface, she seemingly wanted him there when she denounced him before Achashverosh, but she could have spoken with the king privately on this matter. Many rabbinic opinions ensue. R. Eliezer says she wanted to trap him, to catch him off guard (citing *Psalms* 69.23). R. Yehoshua states that it is based on a lesson (from *Proverbs* 25.22) she acquired in her youth: when your foe is hungry, feed him. R. Meir doesn't bother with obscure scriptural verses: she wanted him present so that he wouldn't have time to plot a rebellion against the king. R. Yehuda claims that she wanted everything to appear normal and Haman wouldn't prematurely discover that she was Jewish, with the possible consequence of moving his planned Judeicide up in time. R. Nechemya argues that she didn't want the kingdom's Jews to become too confident and stop praying for divine intervention. R. Yose says simply that Esther wanted Haman right there before her (and the king), with the enhanced possibility that she might trigger Haman to do something foolish. R. Shimon ben Menasya suggests that Haman's very presence might arouse God to act against him. R. Yehoshua ben Korcha has a bizarre understanding of this line: Esther planned to smile at Haman, cause the king to suspect hanky-panky, and have them both executed, thereby ending Haman's odious plan. Rabban Gamliel returns us to reality by stating Esther's aim: make sure Haman would be there when accused to his face and then make sure that the king promptly has him executed, before there's time for someone to muddle his thinking on the matter. But Rabban Gamliel also notes that there's one more opinion that takes into account both why Esther wanted Haman invited and why she wanted only him there. That would be R. Eliezer ha-Modai (the Modean): by having a sole invitee (other than the king) be Haman, Esther's plan was to arouse both the king's jealousy and that of the other (uninvited) courtiers. Two more motives for her plan: Rabba simply cites from *Proverbs* (16.18) the famous line: "Pride goes before a fall"—in other words, Haman would be all puffed up which would hopefully lead to his calamitous ruin. Abaye and Rava together cite a verse from *Jeremiah* (51.39) about "preparing a feast," which would set up the object for defeat.

We now have quite an amazing list of possible reasons that Esther invited Haman to a banquet with the king (and no one else). So, which one is it, Rabba bar Avuha asks none other than Elijah (who if anyone should know, it would be he). Elijah offers a diplomatic reply: All the answers provided by these Tannaim and Amoraim played a role in her thinking.

The exegesis of the *Megilla* skips ahead a few verses to 5.11. This passage follows Haman's walking past Mordechai without the latter so much as acknowledging him. Haman was very bitter but nonetheless went home and bragged about his personal great wealth and all his sons, presumably to quash his humiliation. How many sons, asks the Gemara, did he actually have. We know from the end of the *Megilla* that he had ten given the recounting in the text of their fates (verses 9.7–10). However, that never stops the Gemara from speculation, and Rava gets the ball rolling by saying he actually had thirty sons: ten died, ten were hanged (at the end of the story), and ten were desperately poor beggars. The sages, playing a little fast and loose with a scriptural verse (*I Samuel* 2.5), say that the actual number of these mendicant sons was seventy. Rami bar Abba offers the most outlandish number: 208. He establishes this via *gematria* on "and the large number" (*ve-rov*). The Gemara checks Rami bar Abba's calculation and says the correct numerical value should be 214, when the initial letter *vav* spells the word fully, despite its absence in the text. Rav Nachman bar Yitzchak says, basically: true but the verse has no *vav*, so 208 is the number. But, really, 208 sons?

The exposition of the *Megilla* moves to the beginning of the next chapter (6) where we learn that Achashverosh had a rough night with little sleep. The Gemara cites a number of sources about what that might mean. R. Tanchum suggests that it was really God's sleep (as it were) that was broken up. The sages tells us that the angels were also disturbed, and perhaps it was they who caused the king's fitful night. Rava makes the wild suggestion that the verse might actually be referring to Achashverosh's sleep itself: he started thinking, preventing him from sleeping, how odd it was for his consort to request Haman at a banquet and that they were plotting against him, but then he calmed down because someone, he reasoned, would out of love have informed him of such a heinous, regicidal plot. Before he falls back asleep, he thought that maybe someone had actually performed for him a kindness which he had not rewarded: so maybe that's why people never advise me of plots. So, what does he do? He calls for his retainers to bring in the annals of the kingdom, which are then read aloud to him. There (verse 6.2) he is reminded in this oral presentation of Mordechai's saving his life by reporting the plot of Bigtan and Teresh. The verbal form of the verb "to write" indicates that this had only just been written down, which would mean

16a

Shimshai, the royal scribe and noted Jew-hater, had erased Mordechai's good deed from the annals. How did it find its way back in? The angel Gavriel entered it back into the records.

It is at this point in the *Megilla* (verse 6.3), although not explicitly mentioned here in the Gemara, that Achashverosh asks his retainers what reward was bestowed on this Mordechai fellow. The Gemara does note their reply: Nothing. Rava inserts that they didn't do this out of any love for Mordechai but out of loathing for Haman. The *Megilla* continues (6.4) as Haman enters court with plans to inform the king of his intention to hang Mordechai; the text actually says: "He [Haman] had prepared for him." The last two words, "for him," are superfluous and thus available for interpretation, according to the rules of Talmudic exegesis, and one sage explains that this accentuates the fact that Haman himself would be hanged from the very gallows being prepared for Mordechai.

The kings proceeds to query Haman on how to reward a loyal and trustworthy subject. Thinking, as was his wont, that Achashverosh meant him (Haman), the latter fills several verses (6.7–9) detailing the appropriate honors. He concludes by suggesting such a man ride on a horse belonging to the king through Shushan. Then, Haman is stunned when the king (6.10) hastens him to secure such a horse and do all the things Haman has just laid out, only not for Haman but for his enemy, Mordechai. Achashverosh identifies Mordechai with the appositive phrase: "the Jew." The Gemara has Haman playing dumb and asking the king: which one; there are lots of Jewish men named Mordechai. The king replies that he means the Mordechai at the royal gate. The Gemara has this all as part of the king's instructions to Haman, not as a dialogue. It even adds Haman asking if maybe it would be enough just to give this Mordechai fellow some part of the kingdom from which to collect taxes. The king says: sure, add it to the list of honors. What the *Megilla* (still 6.10) actually does say and which the Gemara repeats is the king instructing Haman not to skip any of the suggestions just laid out.

Disgruntled, to say the least, Haman (verse 6.11) collects the beautiful clothing and horse that he himself has suggested to the king and goes looking for Mordechai. The Gemara report his finding him sitting with a group of sages and explaining to them the laws of *kemitza* (see glossary), a complex ritual from Temple times. Mordechai observes Haman approaching with a horse and fears for his life, justifiably so, and he urges the sages to back away or they might enjoy the same murderous fate awaiting him. Mordechai then dons his shawl and begins praying.

Haman waits for Mordechai to finish his prayers. While doing so, he asks the other men there what they were discussing, and they explain the *kemitza* offering, involving a handful of flour gathering in a complicated manner, that was brought to the Altar when the Temple was standing. Haman retorts that their fistful of flour has apparently displaced his 10,000 talents of silver (see discussion above of *Megilla* 3.9 on *daf* 13b) regarding a plan to eradicate the Jewish people. Mordechai hears this, somehow knows that Haman made such a suggestion to the king, and blurts out to Haman's face that he is "evil" (*rasha*). And, he doesn't stop there, but goes on to claim that no slave can own property, and since Haman was formerly (allegedly) Mordechai's slave, that 10,000 talents was not Haman's to give away.

So, Haman gets Mordechai to dress up in the lovely garb that Haman himself had proposed (with himself in mind) and has his nemesis mount the royal equine. Oddly, Mordechai demurs, saying that he first has to get a bath and a haircut, as it would be unfitting to dress in such fine clothing in such an unclean state. While this was going on, Esther was running around (or having her maidservants run around) to close all the bathhouses and barbershops. Seems counter-intuitive, but the plan was that Haman would then be forced to bring his arch nemesis to a bath, wash him, and then rush home for a pair of scissors to personally cut Mordechai's hair—adding insult to injury. Haman apparently cuts himself on his own scissors and moans; when Mordechai asks what he's complaining about, Haman despondently responds that the man who was once the king's favorite has been reduced to bathhouse attendant and barber. Mordechai again blurts out *rasha*, this time adding that he was once a lowly barber in the town of Kartzum. And, the Gemara marshals a *baraita* that confirms Haman's twenty-two years of haircutting service in Kartzum.

So, Haman cleans Mordechai up, dresses him as instructed, and directs him to mount the royal steed. Mordechai replies that his three days of fasting has seriously weakened him, so he needs help to get up on the horse. Utterly humiliated, Haman bends over and Mordechai actually uses Haman's back as a step stool to mount, kicking Haman in the process. Knowing Hebrew scripture as he does, Haman quotes *Proverbs* (24.17) about the injunction not to exult in an enemy's collapse—that is, where do you get off kicking me when I'm down? Mordechai's rabbinic answer is that the verse from *Proverbs* was meant only for a Jewish enemy; more appropriate here, Mordechai continues, would be *Deuteronomy* 33.29: "And you shall tread on their high places." Mordechai is clearly rubbing it in and apparently enjoying it.

None of the foregoing story of Haman taking Mordechai to get cleaned up or preparing him for his ride through the city is anywhere in the *Megilla*. However, the entire next verse (6.11) is: Haman declares as he parades Mordechai through the streets that such is the honor befitting someone who has earned royal favors. The Gemara adds a particularly nasty tale at this point. We are told that, as her father was leading the horse astride which sat Mordechai, Haman's daughter was watching from high on a rooftop. Not privy to Achashverosh's instructions to her father, she assumed it was her father on the horse and Mordechai leading it; thus confusing the two men, she threw her full chamber pot on the head of the man on the ground beside the horse. He looks up, she sees what she's done, and she falls off the roof to her death. The *Megilla* (verse 6.12) does state that, when this parade concluded, Mordechai went back to his post by the royal gate, and Haman rushed home in mourning with his head covered. Without this business about the daughter, one might think that he was hiding his head in mourning his own abysmal fate, but Rav Sheshet informs us that he was actually mourning his daughter, and the reason he covered his head was the filth she had deposited there.

The *Megilla* (6.13) proceeds to describe how Haman reports to his wife Zeresh and his closest friends all that has just happened, and they advise him to desist. The Gemara asks why those "friends" are referred to that way, but when they offer advice, the Gemara calls them "sages." R. Yochanan answers that, if someone (anyone, even a gentile) says something "wise," that someone is deemed a "wise man" (or woman, presumably). Their advice, not cited in the Gemara but known to every educated reader, was not to fight Mordechai, for if he is really a Jew, you can't win. How could they not know that he was Jewish? The Gemara thus assumes that Haman and Co. believed that one can defeat some of the tribes of Israel, and Mordechai must have come from one of those. So, the unwritten part of their counsel to Haman was that he might triumph over Mordechai, unless he happens to come from one the tribes of Judah, Benjamin, Ephraim, or Menashe.

How would these wise friends of Haman have known specifically which tribes it is wise to avoid? The Gemara assumes everyone, Jew and gentile alike, is fully knowledgeable of Scripture. Their evidence for Judah comes from *Genesis* (49.8); for the other three from *Psalms* (80.3). Inasmuch we have already (see *daf* 12b) established Mordechai's lineage bona fides as both Benjamin and Judah, Haman wouldn't stand a chance. The Hebrew verse in 6.13 uses a double verbal form, and R. Yehuda bar Ilai explains that the nation of Israel is like both dust and stars; when it is defeated, it falls to the earth like so much dust, but when it rises (as with Mordechai at this point in time), it ascends to the stars. In other words, Haman, your demise is certain and will be dreadful.

Lest we forget that Esther has planned a banquet for Haman that evening, just at this point in our story (*Megilla* 6.14) royal retainers arrive chez Haman to rush him to the palace, somewhat confused perhaps from these advisors' words, perhaps as well not having had sufficient time to clean up from his late daughter's mishap. So, the king arrives with Haman, and he asks his lovely bride what she had wished to say. She now unloads on Haman (verse 7.4) and tells the king that Haman cares not a whit about what loss the king might suffer, for it was Haman, after all, who caused Vashti's downfall and had her put to death. Back on *daf* 12b, the Gemara identified the culprit who turned Vashti in as Memuchan, but it also noted that Memuchan was merely another name for Haman. Now, claims Esther, this wicked man wants me dead, too.

Esther has not yet mentioned who this wicked man is, so the king asks her (7.5). She replies (7.6) that it is none other than the fellow right here, the guy with whom you came to this banquet: Haman. Achashverosh becomes understandably enraged (7.7), gets up and walks out to his royal garden to try to calm down (perhaps), but in the next verse (7.8) he returns to the palace still quite angry. What was it about his brief trip to the garden that would not allow his ire to relent? Well, the Gemara tells us that in the garden he saw angels, dressed up as men, pulling the trees up by their roots; when he asks them what they're doing, they reply that Haman told them to do destroy the garden.

Later in the same verse, when the king returns, he espies Haman falling flat on the very couch where Esther was seated. We know from the previous verse that, when the king rose and went out to his garden, Haman turned to beg Esther to spare his life. R. Elazar explains that Haman had tried to get up, but an angel—there seem to be a fair number of them involved in the story—shoved him back down, so that when the king returned, he thinks Haman was trying to attack her. Achashverosh now puts two and two together: the same guy who is destroying my garden outside is trying to destroy me here inside. If the king wasn't angry enough before, this fuels the flames.

Just at this point (*Megilla* 7.9), enter a royal retainer named Charbona who reports that Haman has built a huge scaffold at his home with plans to hang Mordechai on it. The king immediately commands Haman to that very gallows. R. Elazar informs us that this Charbona had been an accomplice of Haman's, which is why he knew details of the immense scaffolding, but he quickly surmised that he had been betting on the wrong horse and switched to Mordechai's side. Haman is promptly hanged by the neck until dead, and only then (7.10) does the king's wrath subside.

The Gemara digresses at this point to explicate *Genesis* 45.22, the story in which Joseph gives his brothers gifts after they find him, a prefiguring of sorts for Mordechai's ultimate triumph. The Gemara wonders about the motivation involved here.

16b

The Gemara begins this thread by citing Rav, via two others, who delineates the famous coat (of many colors) that Jacob gave his favorite son, Joseph, that inspired such jealousy among his brothers. If showing favoritism in this way was a bad move on Jacob's part, why would Joseph years later do something of similar bad judgment by giving Benjamin a gift much nicer than what he gave the others. R. Binyamin bar Yefet states that, in presenting his brother Benjamin with five outfits, he was hinting that in the future his distant tribal offspring would similarly be lauded by a king with kingly garb, as Mordechai would do (*Megilla* 8.15).

Slightly earlier in *Genesis* (45.14), the Torah speaks of Joseph "falling on Benjamin's neck and crying." Scripture, though, has plural "necks." How many could Benjamin have had? R. Elazar explains that this is a metaphor for the two Temples which were to be found in future on Benjaminite terrain and which would also be destroyed. When the verse continues with Benjamin crying on Joseph's neck (singular), this is a reference to the Tabernacle that stood temporarily at Shiloh—on Joseph's terrain—and which would also be demolished. Two verses earlier (45.12), Joseph used other body organs in addressing his brothers, when he exclaims that their eyes see things just like those of brother Ben; the idea here, according to R. Elazar again, is that just as Benjamin was not part of having sold Joseph and for whom he feels no bitterness, he has the same equanimity for all those brothers who did take part.

A few verses later in *Genesis* (45.23), Joseph sends his father Jacob donkeys carrying the "best things of Egypt." The Gemara wants to know what this means. Again, R. Binyamin bar Yefet speaks up in the name of R. Elazar that it means aged wine, something older folks find agreeable. Joseph had sworn no lingering ill feeling for his brethren, but when Jacob passed away, they suspected things for them might change. They come before him (50.18) apparently anxious about their future. This corresponds, according to R. Binyamin bar Yefet in the name of R. Elazar, to the adage: when the fox has its hour (is in the ascendant), bow down before it. (I'm guessing that a fox does not qualify as an idol.) Comparing Joseph to a lowly fox strikes the Gemara as highly unfair, so it tries to wriggle out of such a perspective. Joseph's effort to calm their anxious nerves isn't working with alacrity, so (50.21) he tries a little harder and "speaks to their hearts." This apparently does the trick.

The Gemara now returns to the *Megilla* and verse 8.16 records the Jews utter exuberance at the execution of Haman. It expresses this exuberance with four words and then the Gemara takes each of them apart for exegesis: "light" denotes Torah (*Proverbs* 6.23 states explicitly: "Torah is light") and means that the Jews were allowed to study it; "gladness" denotes a holiday and means that Jews may be glad on their holiday (*Deuteronomy* 16.14); "joy" denotes the mitzvah of circumcision, citing *Psalms* (119.162) in a manner too obscure to reconstruct; and "honor" denotes the mitzvah of *tefillin* and cites *Deuteronomy* (28.10) which speaks of God's name being "upon you." R. Eliezer the Great notes a *baraita* which makes special mention here of the head *tefillin*. Allegedly, all of the mitzvot to which Jews were now able once again to perform had been outlawed under Haman.

Celebrating the downfall of an evil man and the demise of his devastating plans is one thing, but the *Megilla* in chapter 9 lays out Mordechai's extraordinary rise and the merciless extinguishing of those who had sought his and his people's destruction; verse 9.6 mentions some 500 enemies who were slain in Shushan alone. Verses 9.7–9 names each of the ten sons of Haman. These three verses are very short, little more than their proper names; the first word of verse 9.10 is *aseret* 'ten,' and the reader of the *Megilla* is instructed that he must articulate verses 9.7–9 through *aseret* in verse 9.10 all in one breath. Why? They all died at the same moment. R. Yochanan adds to this gruesome scene by stating that pronunciation of the letter *vav* in name of Haman's son Vaizata should be lengthened like a pole used by boatmen to navigate on a river. Why? Because all ten sons were hanged from the same long pole.

The Gemara chooses to insert a curious point here about the way the text of the *Megilla* is written, what it calls a half-brick above a whole brick and a whole brick above a half. "Brick" refers here to a block of text, and the style of transcription is said to typify songs of praise. The style has an uneven, almost rickety appearance which is basic to its alleged meaning—the wicked should never gain sound footing.

In verse 9.12, the king reports to Esther that they're mopping up the plotters and some 500 of the latter have bit the dust in the capital; and one can only imagine the number of those put to the sword in the provinces (actually, verse 9.16 puts the number at 75,000). R. Abbahu interjects that at this point yet another angel intercedes and smacks the king on the mouth, because he was initially coming in anger to report the excessive killing—there is not a hint of this mood in the *Megilla*, but Achashverosh then asks Esther what her wish was that he had promised to grant.

The Gemara next jumps ahead a few verses, as verse 9.30 notes that communications were dispatched to each of the 127 provinces (see *daf* 11a) of Achashverosh's kingdom: "words of peace and truth." This phrase, according to either R. Tanchum or R. Assi, means that the *Scroll of Esther* has to be written with etched lines on parchment like the Torah itself. The Jews are now (9.31) instructed by Mordechai and Esther to observe the Purim holiday.

Mordechai (*Megilla* 10.3) is now the king's #2 man and a great favorite of the Jewish people for whom he looked out. The text actually says his popularity extended to the "multitude of his brethren." That would seem to imply that a minority were dissatisfied. Who might they be? The Gemara states they were some of his former Sanhedrin colleagues. Their problem with the heroic figure of our story? By becoming such a high official in the kingdom, he undoubtedly was derelict in Torah study. Some people are never satisfied! Rav Yosef makes a stark statement in this context: Torah study is more important that saving lives. This would seem to contradict the commandment to preserve life at all (actually, almost all) cost, so the Gemara's point must be that, once Haman and all the thousands of bad guys were gone, he still chose to serve under Achashverosh because of possible future threats, not imminent ones, to the Jewish people.

Torah study itself is sufficiently important to warrant a digression. It was either Rav or Rav Shmuel bar Marta who averred that Torah study supersedes the erection of the Temple, and he offers a proof concerning Ezra's continued study of Torah and postponing *Aliya* (moving to the Holy Land). Rabba reports another's teaching to the effect that Torah study is more important than honoring one's parents, and he offers a proof concerning Jacob's elongated period of study while ignoring his folks.

17a

This leads to an extraordinary digression calculating the number of years Jacob studied in the Academy of Ever, while apparently ignoring his parents.

The first step in this rabbit hole is to note the explicit mention in *Genesis* (25.17) that Ishmael lived a full 137 years, a fact the Gemara remarks is stated in scripture, to work out the number of years Jacob lived.

So, then, Ishmael was fourteen years older than his brother Isaac; we know this from comparing the recording of their father's ages (86–100) between his two sons' births. That was relatively easy. We also know from *Genesis* (25.26) that Isaac was sixty when his baby twins were born. That would mean that Ishmael was seventy-four when his nephews were born. And, in addition, that would mean that he still has sixty-three years to go. Simple reasoning makes Jacob sixty-three at the time of Ishmael's death. Jacob receives a paternal blessing at this point and soon thereafter must take refuge with his Uncle Laban. We know he spent fourteen years there, and then Joseph was born to a seventy-seven years old father. *Genesis* (41.46) states that this same Joseph was thirty years of age when he "stood before Pharaoh." Although they had not yet been reunited, Jacob would have been 107 at the time. When Jacob did come to Egypt, seven famous years of great harvests followed by two famine years had passed—the latter was, in fact, the reason he and his sons migrated there—and that would mean he was a whopping 116 years of age.

But, wait, we may have a problem, for when Pharaoh asks Jacob directly how old he is, Jacob bluntly replies 130 (*Genesis* 47.8–9). What about those missing fourteen years? What was he doing during that time? The Gemara claims that those were the fourteen years, between leaving Isaac and reaching Laban in Aram Naharaim, that are missing. These are the same fourteen years that he was studying at the Academy of Ever. A *baraita* seals the deal by stating unequivocally that Jacob secreted himself at the Academy in question for fourteen years.

Accepting its own calculations, the Gemara asks now if there is any proof that Jacob was not chastised for ignoring the commandment to honor his parents? A *baraita* has it that, after his brothers sold him, Joseph did not see his father for twenty-two years (seventeen year old at the time of sale and thirty when he became Pharaoh's majordomo [meaning thirteen years of absence] + seven years of good harvests + two years of famine = twenty-two.) By contrast, Jacob himself was out of touch with his own parents for thirty-six years. What accounts for the difference here? It was that fourteen years (36−22=14) that he spent in Ever's Academy. Chapter One comes to a conclusion with a little more calculation, but let's leave it there and move onto new terrain.

Notes

1. Virtually the identical phrase can be found at *Chagiga* 10a.

2. Described somewhat more fully in tractate *Zevachim* 119a. See my *(Sacrifices) Left at the Altar: Reading Tractate* Zevachim *of the Babylonian Talmud* (Lanham: Hamilton Books, 2014), pp. 324–25.

3. *Menachot* 109b; see my *Grains of Truth: Reading Tractate* Menachot *of the Babylonian Talmud* (Lanham: Hamilton Books, 2014), pp. 369–70.

4. A Jewish mother gives her son two ties for a birthday present; when he next visits her for Shabbat dinner, he decides to wear one of them to show how much he appreciated her gift; so, he rings the doorbell, she comes to open the door, and when she sees him wearing the tie, she exclaims: "So, you didn't like the other tie?"

Chapter 2

Properly Reading the *Megilla*

17a (cont'd)

The first Mishna of this chapter covers a lot of ground. It begins by stating starkly that, if one reads parts of the *Megilla* out of their proper order, one has failed to fulfill the mitzvah to read or hear the text read. Similarly, recitation from memory or reading it in Aramaic translation ("*targum*") or any language but Hebrew fails to fulfill the mitzvah. Why Aramaic is separated from the other foreign languages is curious, and the rabbis tell us that it enjoys a status not on a par with Hebrew but certainly higher than any other foreign tongue. The Mishna now makes an exception: the *Megilla* may be read for foreigners, those who do not understand the original Hebrew text, if it is read from a scroll written in a language those foreigners do understand. Oddly, if someone who does not understand Hebrew hears the *Megilla* read from a scroll transcribed in Ashurit script (see *dapim* 8b-9a), he nonetheless has fulfilled the mitzvah.

It is also fine if the reader breaks up his recitation with pauses or reads while verging on sleep. Another interesting case is the scribe who is writing a *Megilla* or expounding on every word in it, or actually correcting it; if he does this assiduously and intones every word of the text, he has fulfilled the mitzvah. If he is less than completely persevering in this regard, he has not as yet fulfilled the mitzvah.

If the text was written with one of an assortment of materials to be defined on the following *dapim* (18b-19a), reading such a *Megilla* does not satisfy one's mitzvah. It has to be written in Ashurit script on parchment with black ink. Ashurit insures it will be in Hebrew, of course, and that means hearing such a scroll read thusly works for everyone; if written in a foreign language, that only works for that segment of the audience which understands that foreign tongue.

Lots to work with here. The Gemara begins plaintively with a simple question: How do we know all this stuff in the Mishna? It starts with the question of reading pieces of the *Megilla* out of order. Rava cites the *Megilla* itself (verse 9.27) where, toward the end of the story, the Jews agree to commemorate (celebrate) their delivery from the edge of death at Haman's hands: according to "their writing" and "their correct time every year." He notes that just as "their correct time"—Adar 14 and 15—must be in sequence (how could Adar 15 precede Adar 14?), the reading of the text must be. Accepting nothing at face value, the Gemara retorts that there is no mention of "reading" here; the verse in question only refers to celebrating. In fact, the very next verse (9.28) states that these two days shall henceforth be "remembered and celebrated." By placing these two terms next to one another, this verse compares them; we can't very well remember the two days out of order, and thus the celebration (namely, reading the *Megilla*) similarly must be in its proper order.

Correct sequential reading apparently peaks the interest of the Gemara and leads to a lengthy digression. One sage offers the view that the following prayers also have to be recited in proper order: *Hallel* (see *daf* 14a), comprised of *Psalms* 113–118; the *Shema*; and the *Shemone Esrei* ("eighteen," the silent and standing prayer that is central to all daily prayers). Rabba steps up to note that early in *Hallel* itself (*Psalms* 113.3), there is mention of the rising and setting of the sun; just as this order can't be inverted, ditto the prayer of praise to God (*Hallel*). Rav Yosef corroborates this with a citation from the other end of *Hallel* (*Psalms* 118.24) which notes that God has made "the day," and its hourly order cannot be inverted in any way—so, too, *Hallel*. Rav Avya jumps on this bandwagon to cite the word *yehi* 'shall be' from *Psalms* 113.2, referring to blessing the name of God; the implication is that it always will be thus, just as it is. Finally, either Rav Nachman bar Yitzchak or R. Acha bar Yaakov cite from the same verse "from this time and forever," indicating that *Hallel* will never change.

Let's move on to the *Shema*. A *baraita* from R. Yehuda ha-Nasi teaches us that reciting the three paragraphs that constitute the *Shema* must be precisely as they are written. Other sages demur and state that it can be read in any language at all. The Gemara asks on what R. Yehuda ha-Nasi bases his view. One word in the *Shema* (Deuteronomy 6.6) reads:

17b

vehayu 'and they shall be'; the implication is that this refers to the *Shema* itself: as it is now, so it should always remain, in Hebrew. The sages tell us that, as its name indicates, the first word of this prayer, *shema*, means "hear," and the suggestion is that one may hear it in any language. How does R.

Yehuda ha-Nasi deal with the sages' thesis about hearing? He would argue that the individual must recite the *Shema* so that that individual hears what he has recited. The sages don't agree here, as they would judge an inaudible *Shema* nonetheless fulfilling the mitzvah.

Now, turning to the sages, how are they to rationalize *vehayu*? Doesn't this mean that the *Shema* should forever and always be heard in Hebrew? The sages now use this term as an indication that the order of verses in the prayer be recited just as they are. Meanwhile, R. Yehuda ha-Nasi needs an explanation for the issue of sequence. He points to the word *hadevarim* 'the words' which the *Shema* uses rather than simply *devarim* 'words' as a way of indicating specific words (and not any reordering of them). The sages don't see this as particularly important.

The Gemara then tries to extract teachings for each of the two contestants here. Does R. Yehuda ha-Nasi's view lead to the fact that we may read the whole Torah in any language we choose? This seems a little strange and is promptly rejected. By contrast, is this what the sages are after? Again, this avenue is blocked.

Now, on to the *Shemone Esrei* and why it, too, must be read in proper order. A *baraita* is invoked which states that one Shimon Hapakuli is the man responsible for arranging these eighteen blessings which he did at the behest of Rabban Gamliel in Yavne. R. Yochanan (or maybe it was a *baraita*) has another view: these blessings were fixed by 120 (there's that number again) elders (meaning the Men of the Great Assembly), among them a fair number of prophets.

The Gemara now enters into an analysis of the sequence of these eighteen blessings. A heads up here: there are actually nineteen. So why do we start by blessing the patriarchs (*avot*)? Because of the accumulated qualities of Abraham, Isaac, and Jacob, God vowed to assist the Jewish people in history. The Gemara says that we need bless them because of *Psalm* 29.1, which refers to the "sons of the mighty ones," and the Gemara understands "the mighty ones" as the forefathers. The next blessing is about "God's might" (*gevurot*) and the same psalm is cited as a reason for reciting it here. The third blessing in the sequence is about "God's holiness" (*kedushot*) and the same psalm, next verse (29.2) is the rationale.

The fourth blessing concerns "insight (*bina*)," and the Gemara asks why it should follow that of "God's holiness." Here we are referred to two consecutive verses in *Isaiah* (29.23–24). The former instructs us to sanctify and revere God; the latter teaches that "those who err in spirit" will come to "know insight." Then, why would the blessing of "repentance" (*teshuva*) follow "insight"? We turn for explication to an earlier verse in *Isaiah* (6.10) where one's heartfelt understanding will surely lead one to repent of one's sins and then heal. True that, but why then isn't the next blessing in the cycle "healing" (*refua*), and why does "forgiveness" (*selicha*) come next instead? Bite your tongue, the Gemara states in so many words, citing a later verse in *Isaiah* (55.7), which dictates return to God (i.e., repentance), Who will then forgive. So, forgiveness must precede healing. The Gemara's not done with questioning the order here, for *Psalms* has a pair of verses (103.3–4) teaching that God first forgives, then heals, and then redeems. Shouldn't healing come right after repentance? The Gemara already cited it, but *Psalms* 6.10 states clearly that the sinner repents and is then healed: QED.

Why is the seventh blessing "redemption" (*geula*) and not "healing"? Rava explains that, because Israel's destiny is to be redeemed in the seventh year, *geula* occupies this spot. The "redemption" referred to in this blessing does not mean the ultimate liberation of the Jewish nation, but rather redemption from the *tsores* of quotidian life. Nonetheless, given the name *geula*, the sages afforded it pride of seventh place. OK, and then why is "healing" placed after it in spot eight? R. Acha has an ingenious answer. It's a reference to circumcision which occurs on the eighth day of a male child's life and which also necessitates healing. How did the "blessing of the years" (*birkat hashanim*) find itself ninth? R. Aleksandri claims that this blessing is aimed at those evil sorts who target the poor and raise food prices. When David wrote the *Psalms*, he made his condemnation of such sorts ninth, hence its place here.

Next up is another important one, "ingathering of exiles" (*kibutz galuyot*). The Gemara asks why it follows the "blessing of the years," and a verse from *Ezekiel* (36.8) is invoked indicating that the ingathering will follow plentiful harvests. The next blessing is the "restoration of justice" (*din*); with the exiles back on the Land, judgment time for those evil sorts arrives. The verse used here is once again from *Isaiah* (1.25) and speaks of purging scum. This is followed by the "blessing regarding the heretics" (*birkat haminim*); with the evil ones out of the way now, other sinners and heretics will cease to exist—à la *Isaiah* 1.28.

We come now to the "righteous ones" (*tsadikim*). With evil, wicked, sinning, and heretical types out of the picture, it's time for the righteous (including, we are told, the righteous converts, a fascinating group in their own right throughout history). Why, pray tell, do we have to wait all the way to place fourteen for the blessing for the "[re]building of Jerusalem" (*binyan Yerushalaim*)? Because, with the rise of the righteous in the previous blessing, all the better prepared will we be to ring out their glory in the capital of the Land of Israel? With the exiles ingathered, the heretics and their ilk removed, justice restored, harvests bountiful, the righteous in the ascendant, and Jerusalem rebuilt, it must be time to reinstate the "kingdom of David" (*malchut bet David*).

18a

The Gemara invokes a straightforward verse to support this placement, as *Hosea* (3.5) states that, with the Israelites back on the Land, they can now seek out God and David.

Next in order is the blessing for "acceptance of prayer" (*kabalat tefila*). The Gemara cites an obscurely "related" verse from *Isaiah* (56.7) about God moving the people to "His holy mountain" and only then having them construct a prayer house; it interprets this as first a king (David) and then the Temple. This is followed by the prayer for the Temple "service" (*avoda*); in other words, once prayer has been accepted, it can now be offered preferably at the Temple (someday). A later passage in the same verse from *Isaiah* is cited about offerings at the Altar. Number eighteen is the "thanksgiving" (*hodaa*) blessing: thanks offered to God once the Temple is back, regular prayer is reinstituted, and all the preceding are in place. A supporting verse from *Psalms* (50.23) is cited in which thanks to God follows the donation of a sacrificial offering.

That concludes the eighteen blessings, but the Gemara continues by asking why the "thanksgiving" blessing is followed by the "blessing of the priests" (*birkat hakohanim*). The Gemara quotes a supportive verse from *Leviticus* (9.22) which speaks of Aaron blessing the people. But, a careful reading of that verse would seem to indicate that Aaron's blessing actually preceded a series of sacrifices he carried out; why, then, does the priestly blessing not immediately come before the *avoda*? An even more careful reading of the verse indicates that, while mention of Aaron's sacrifices follows his blessing, he actually carried out those sacrifices before offering the blessing. OK, then, why doesn't it immediately follow the *avoda*? Answer: the "thanksgiving" blessing is effectively twinned with the Temple "service" (in that order)—only then can the priestly blessing be intoned.

Finally, how is it that all this is followed by the "peace" (*shalom*) blessing? Perhaps, the bigger question here is why the priestly blessing and this last one are in this order at all. The former is usually not part of the *Shemone Esrei*, and the *shalom* prayer would be number nineteen (and it is). The Gemara will have to account for this. In any event this is the order for the prayers that the Men of the Great Assembly forged. Actually, they selected the blessing, and their order for them was forgotten; it was the aforementioned Shimon Hapakuli who put them back in proper sequence.

Once these blessings and the order for reciting them were fixed, these were established as such for all time, with no additions or subtractions. The rabbis were quite adamant about the adding business. They apparently wanted things kept under control in prayer. Thus, R. Yochanan (as reported by Rabba bar bar Chana) condemns excessive devotion to God and says such a person will be "uprooted from the world" (citing a verse from *Job* [37.20] which has to be creatively interpreted). One R. Yehuda (not the one most frequently cited in the Talmud) actually invokes *Psalms* 62.5: "Silence in praise for You." This can't mean no praise at all, but it does mean silence is better than excess. We next encounter the appearance of Rav Dimi, a frequent traveled from the Land of Israel to Babylonia who relates how people in the former treat a given issue, and he recounts that in the Land they have a saying that, if a word is worth a *sela* (a coin), then silence is worth two.

And, suddenly we are back to discussing the *Megilla*. The Mishna stated that reciting it from memory does not fulfill the mitzvah. How do we know this? Rava offers a *gezera shava* (see above, 2b) for the word "commemoration": *Megilla* 9.28 and *Exodus* 17.14. The former sets the days for celebrating-commemorating the holiday of Purim on which the *Megilla* is read; the latter relates God's directive to Moses to write down "in a book" a record of Amalek's attack on the children of Israel. Thus, the commemoration is about a book. The Gemara then offers a fairly trivial counter argument. Yes, a book, but does that necessarily mean "reading" from it? Of course, it does, and the Gemara cites *Deuteronomy* (25.17, 19) wherein scripture instructs us to "remember" (*zachor*) and not to forget: Amalek. The mind can on occasion be fickle, even forgetful, and therefore "reading" is demanded.

The Mishna also noted that reading the *Megilla* in Aramaic translation was not a proper fulfillment of the mitzvah. How so? The practice of eyeing the Hebrew text and translating into Aramaic is no different, according to the Gemara, than reciting from memory. What if the text of the *Megilla* was written down in Aramaic, and the reader read what was before him?—no good, because Aramaic is not Hebrew. Yet, the Mishna seemed to have a special provision for foreigners, that they could read the *Megilla* in any language. How does that jibe with the injunction that it must be read in Hebrew? Rav and Shmuel actually agree on this one, insisting that "foreign language" here refers to Greek (and only Greek). What's going on here? If the reader has a Hebrew text before him and he intones in Greek, this is no different from the case above of reciting the text from memory. R. Acha (in the name of R. Elazar) states what has to be the proper meaning here: the *Megilla* in question must have been written in Greek. As long as we have one line of argument from R. Acha (in the name of R. Elazar), the Gemara suggests we shouldn't pass up the opportunity for another, but it is so completely unrelated to the discussion at hand that I shall not step foot into this rabbit hole.

The rabbis apparently are unhappy with Rav and Shmuel's take on Greek as the only possible or legitimate foreign language in which to intone the *Megilla*. And, a *baraita* rules out several "languages," including Greek, for fulfillment of the mitzvah. The Gemara seems to come to their defense: if people only understand one of the languages in question, including Greek, and the *Megilla* is read in that one language, then the mitzvah is properly observed. The question remains as to why Rav and Shmuel only mentioned Greek and not other languages. The point is not that Rav and Shmuel were limiting the opening up of fulfillment of the mitzvah to Greek, even if one didn't know that language. This contradicts the *baraita* which said Greek language to (monolingual) Greeks is fine, but for anyone else it fails to fulfill the mitzvah.

Now, Rav and Shmuel, we learn, stated their view based on a teaching of Rabban Shimon ben Gamliel (see 8b) that the only foreign language in which scripture might be written down was Greek. Rabban Shimon then elevated Greek to a par with Hebrew, while the rabbis of the *baraita* relegated it fit only for Greek speakers. The Gemara asks then why Rav and Shmuel didn't just claim that the *halacha* accords with Rabban Shimon ben Gamliel—that would have saved us some time; so, as with other books of Scripture, so too with the *Megilla*. This issue has dissipated with time, as ancient Greek is no longer in contention as an appropriate language for reading the *Megilla*.

The flip side of all this is someone who hear the *Megilla* read in Hebrew but doesn't himself understand the language. The Mishna says he's fulfilled the mitzvah. The Gemara asks an obvious question: how can the mitzvah be fulfilled, if the person in question has no understanding of what was intoned? The Gemara basically offers a non-answer: it's comparable to women (who are usually unschooled) and unschooled men, both categories being people who fulfill the mitzvah despite not knowing the language in which the *Megilla* is being read. Ravina pulls a halachic rabbit out of his yarmulke. He points out that there are words and phrases in the *Megilla* (e.g., 8.10) that no one understands, so the mitzvah is not understanding each and every word—it's reading the text and publicizing the miracle of Purim.

The Mishna next addresses a reading of the *Megilla* with pauses or is in any way broken up—mitzvah fulfilled. The word used here *seirugin* for "discontinuous" apparently confused the rabbis, but the matter was cleared up by the maidservant for R. Yehuda ha-Nasi, testimony to the great wisdom circulating in his immediate circle (even among the help). This provides grounds for a digression regarding a number of terms, none of them related directly to the *Megilla*. For more such incidents are recorded, and interestingly three of these linguistic conundrums are resolved for them by the same maidservant, the fourth by an Arab who was traveling with Rabba bar bar Chana.

A *baraita* sets the record straight. Reading in a *seirugin* manner—that is, "discontinuously"—is OK.

18b

Reading verses of the *Megilla* out of order is not. R. Muna (in the name of R. Yehuda) offers a clarification: if the reader breaks off and the amount of time that passes before he starts up again is equivalent to the amount of time it would take to read the entire text, he must return to the beginning of the *Megilla*. Rav Yosef states affirmatively that this ruling is *halacha*. But, we needs some details, as Abaye asks for more precision on the length of time: the time from where the reader broke off to the end or from start to finish? Rav Yosef clarifies that the *halacha* refers here to the entire reading, for people theoretically might break off at many different places. The safest general ruling is the whole *Megilla*.

But, now we're in for a really interesting turn of events. R. Abba reports (in the name of R. Yirmeya bar Abba who, in turn, says in the name of Rav) that, yes, R. Muna's ruling was *halacha*. However, Shmuel says it ain't necessarily so—no pause of any length serves to disenfranchise the mitzvah. That may have been true in the city of Sura, he adds, but not in Pumbedita, sites of the two most famous yeshivas in Babylonia; in Pumbedita, the ruling is taught by Rav Kahana in Rav's name that the *halacha* follows R. Muna, but Shmuel claims it is not. There is yet another explanation of the possible confusion: Rav Bivi claims the opposite it the case, with Rav claiming the *halacha* does not accord with R. Muna, and Shmuel claiming that it does. Rav Yosef steps back into the fray and instructs us to follow Rav Bivi's take. He likes it because, when push comes to shove, Shmuel adopts a more stringent ruling.

Moving right along, should a scribe writing a *Megilla* forget to write any letters or verses from the text, then if the reader fills in these blanks from memory, as a synagogue "translator" (*meturgeman*) of old would instinctively translate, the mitzvah is fulfilled. Another *baraita* raises the issue of a *Megilla* with obscured or ripped letters in the parchment text; again, if they are distinguishable, one can read from it and fulfill the mitzvah. However, if they are not distinguishable, no mitzvah. Does this not fly in the face of the previous ruling? "No problem" (*lo kashya*) replies the Gemara, because the *baraita* regarding indecipherable letters actually means an entire or, at least, most of a *Megilla* in that state, while the earlier *baraita* about missing letters (or verses) refers to a spotty issue with the text.

We return now to the issue of reading out of proper order of the text, and a *baraita* teaches as follows: should the reader somehow forget to read a verse, he cannot say that he'll come back after completing the reading and recite that verse; he has to return to that spot in the *Megilla*, recite the missed verse, and continue from that point. A related ruling in the same *baraita*: if someone were to enter shul at the halfway point in the reading of the *Megilla*, he cannot join in for the latter half with the understanding that later he will read the first half; he has to read the text in its proper sequence, start to finish.

Back to the Mishna and the odd acceptance of the mitzvah if one reads the *Megilla* as he is on the verge of dozing off. The Mishna clarifies what is meant by dozing off. Rav Ashi says that it is somewhere between being asleep and being awake. We're speaking here of the actually reader, not listeners in the congregation. Rav Ashi explains a bit further that, if someone calls out to the reader, he is able to acknowledge the shout out, but not necessarily offer a rational reply unless his memory if appropriately jogged.

The next passage in the Mishna refers to the scribe who is writing a *Megilla* or someone explicating the text or someone correcting errors; if one such person concentrates on each and every word in so doing, the mitzvah is fulfilled. Let's take the case of a scribe. He knows a given verse by heart and then writes, that is no different from someone, as we saw above, who recites the text from memory; to fulfill the mitzvah, he has to transcribe the text verse by verse and then read it verse by verse. No, responds R. Chelbo (in the name of Rav Chama bar Gurya who said this in the name of Rav), he's got to read the entire *Megilla* start to finish, and that's the *halacha*. It's even acceptable, he adds, to read from verse 2.5 ("A Jewish man") to the end, an opinion we shall confront on the next *daf* in a new Mishna.

Rabba bar bar Chana next reports a teaching from R. Yochanan that a scribe must do his work by copying from a written text. The Gemara makes quick work of this. It's surely fine to copy from a complete text before one, but it is not the law that not copying is forbidden. The Gemara is not through with rebutting this view. R. Shimon ben Elazar tells a story of one occasion on which R. Meir traveled to Asya (Asia?) to intercalate a month, and finding no available *Megilla*, he wrote one out from memory. This should lay Rabba bar bar Chana's assertion about the necessity of copying to rest. This case is deemed special by R. Abbahu (with help from R. Yirmeya), because R. Meir's level of knowledge was such that he knew the entire Torah by heart. Rav Chisda is now cited for effectively chastising Rav Chananel for copying scriptural books without a master from which to copy, on the understanding that doing so from memory is prohibited. The Gemara notes here that, yes, R. Meir had an exceptional memory, but his case was one in which there was no available *Megilla* from which to read, making it a situation of imperative need that he produce one.

Abaye allowed the house of Bar Chavu to transcribe *tefillin* and mezuzahs without copying. On whose authority? A *baraita* is cited which basically says, for our purposes, that in these instances, no master is necessary. Why? Everyone know the Torah passages contained in *tefillin* and mezuzahs.

When introducing the Mishna upon which we are now elaborating, we skipped naming the kinds of materials one may use to write a *Megilla*. We now begin identifying several difficult terms: *sam* is orpiment; *sikra* (Rabba bar bar Chana says it is more properly *sikrisa*) is vermilion; *kumus* is tree sap;

19a

and *kankantum* is a black substance used by shoemakers; meanwhile, *diftera* is a kind of parchment treated with salt and flour but not gallnuts; and *neyar* is papyrus. In all these cases of "inks" and "parchments," such a *Megilla* is unacceptable to read from and fulfill the mitzvah.

As noted in the Mishna, the *Megilla* text must be written in Ashurit script (Hebrew), as verse 9.27 reads "in the prescribed manner at the proper time each year." Thus, it has to be Hebrew. The Mishna also prescribes for the writing of the text: parchment and with black ink. How do we know this? This time we are invited to another *gezera shava* comparing forms of the word for writing from the *Megilla* (9.29: "Esther wrote") with *Jeremiah* (36.18) where it is explicitly parchment and black ink.

Time for a new Mishna. Back in Chapter One, we addressed the issue of when we are to read the *Megilla* in walled cities (Adar 15) as opposed to towns without walls (Adar 14). This Mishna now deals with a person who ordinarily lives in one of these residential spaces but one year finds himself for a portion of Purim in the other. If someone finds himself in the other space but returns to his normal home space, then he reads the *Megilla* as he would ordinarily. However, should he not return in time, he is to read with his "adopted" community that year. One other issue this Mishna addresses: how much of the *Megilla* read fulfills the mitzvah? That is, do you have to read it all, or from what point counts as an effective execution of the mitzvah? R. Meir says the whole shebang. R. Yehuda (as noted above) says from "A Jewish man" (verse 2.5) till the end. R. Yose offers the most lenient position: from "After these things" (verse 3.1) forward.

The Gemara lets Rava have the first word about occupants of different kinds of populated areas. Speaking of the ordinary resident of a walled city who finds himself in a town without walls but plans to return and read the *Mishna* on Adar 15; he claims that he does, as the Mishna indicates, but only if he gets home by the night of the 14th. If he does not return on the 14th, that means he will still find himself in the unwalled site at the break of day and should read with locals on Adar 14. Rava supports this line of reasoning by demonstrating that one visiting away from home adopts the duties of locals regardless of the length of his stay. He cites the *Megilla* (verse 9.19) which mentions Jews from "unwalled places" who live in "unwalled towns." That strikes Rava as redundant, which means it's available for exegesis. He asserts that a Jew who finds himself in an unwalled place even for a single day is to be seen as a resident of that unwalled site. OK, so having located a scriptural proof to substantiate such an instance, what about the reverse? This time the Gemara turns to logic rather than appealing to Scripture and simply says that if what it has demonstrated works for unwalled places, the same should hold for walled cities.

Back close to the beginning this tractate, the Mishna noted that residents of villages may read the *Megilla*, if necessary, on the preceding assembly day. What if one such villager then found himself in a nearby town on Adar 14? Rava's answer: he reads again with the town folk that day. Why so stringent? The ordinary day on which villagers are obligated to read is Adar 14; the assembly day reading is an alternative offered by the rabbis so these folks would be back in the villages to prepare food and water for the urbanites. So, if a villager had read the *Megilla* on an assembly day and returned to his village by Adar 14 to prepare victuals, he is afforded the leniency of not having to read it a second time. If he's in a town, he must. Abaye objects to Rava's explication and cites a *baraita*, but the Gemara demonstrates that the text of the *baraita* is faulty.

The next part of the Mishna concerns from what point in the text of the *Megilla* must one read to fulfill the mitzvah. The Mishna offered three views, and now it adds a fourth from a *baraita*: R. Shimon ben Yochai states (by far the most lenient view) from verse 6.1 ("That night") to the end, roughly the latter half of the whole text. R. Yochanan claims that all four of our authorities are expounding the same verse in the *Megilla* (9.29) which deals with "acts of power" about which Esther and Mordechai wrote; the question is how our four rabbis understand those words in quotation marks. R. Meir's insistence that entire *Megilla* must be read derives from understanding this term as Achashverosh's power, a topic found throughout the entire text. R. Yehuda's view clearly relates our term with Mordechai's power; thus, one can begin with "A Jewish man" which is where our male hero first assumes a post of importance. R. Yose assesses our term to imply Haman's power, and thus the verse "After these things" (i.e., the king promoted Haman) is a fitting place to start if one cannot attend an entire reading. R. Shimon ben Yochai focuses on the verse starting "That night," because it equates "acts of power" with the miracle of Purim, and it marks the decisive moment in the *Megilla* when the fate of the Jews began to appear safe.

All of the foregoing paragraph was based on R. Yochanan's identification of a source to understand the four rabbis' readings. R. Huna now offers a different perspective based on verse 9.26 which makes the point that recitation of the events commemorated by the *Megilla* must explain why the main actors acted as they did and what ensued accordingly. So, let's see how this works for our four rabbis. R. Meir's view (the whole *Megilla*) would resonate with the king's (mis)understanding that the Temple was gone for good and that he could use its sanctified vessels as he wished. Consequence: killing of Vashti. R. Yehuda's position ("A Jewish man") would resonate with Mordechai's enraging Haman by not bowing down to him. Consequence: a miracle. R. Yose's viewpoint ("After these things") resonates with the cause of Haman's ire vis-à-vis all the Jews: again, it was Mordechai's refusal to bow down before him. Consequence: he and sons are all hanged. Finally, R. Shimon ben Yochai's stance ("That night") resonates with the king's calling upon his retainers to bring him his annals revealing Mordechai had never been properly rewarded for saving the royal personage's life. Consequence: Esther invites Haman to her little banquet, and the miracle of Purim ensues.

So, we have four views on where a minimal reading of the *Megilla* must begin so as to fulfill the mitzvah, and we have two separate explanations for each of these four views. R. Chelbo (in the name of Rav Chama bar Gurya who said in the name of Rav) that the *halacha* must follow R. Meir's ruling that the entire text must be read. As it so often does, the Gemara proceeds to present another view of R. Chelbo (same sequence of authorities): the *Megilla* is described (verse 9.32) as a "book" (*sefer*) and (9.29) as a "letter" (*igeret*). The former means it must be written like a Torah scroll, and if the parchment pieces are sewn together with linen, it is rendered void. Inasmuch as it is also dubbed a "letter," it can be stitched in a distinctive way and be legit.

Rav Yehuda (in Shmuel's name) states that reading a *Megilla* that had been transcribed on parchment scrolls together with other scriptural texts has in fact not fulfilled the mitzvah. Rava modulates this stringency to note that, if a *Megilla* text written in such a manner is considerably shorter or longer than other items on the same scroll, then a reader of said text has indeed fulfilled the mitzvah. Levi bar Shmuel was apparently reading before R. Yehuda a *Megilla*

19b

of this sort, and R. Yehuda outlawed it on the spot. R. Chiyya bar Abba (in R.Yochanan's name) invoked the same ruling as R. Yehuda, but then tempered it by saying that this only holds when one is reading in public.

In another teaching of R. Yochanan's articulated by R. Chiyya bar Abba, we learn that leaving a margin on either side (above and below) the parchment stitches is a tradition Moses received atop Mt. Sinai. This sort of assertion is frequently used to justify a reading when there is no immediate or obvious scriptural verse or logical explanation for an interpretation. In this rare instance, R. Chiyya bar Abba withdrew his assertion and claimed it was a rabbinic enactment to ensure that the parchment does not tear.

Another ruling from the same source: when, at different times, Moses and Elijah found themselves sheltered in a cave, God's divine presence passed over them, and had there been an opening even as small as the eye of a needle, they couldn't have survived the brilliance of the light. One last teaching from R. Chiyya bar Abba (channeling R. Yochanan), in which he clarifies *Deuteronomy* 9.10 which declares that the words inscribed on the second set of tablets accord with everything God imparted to Moses at Sinai. We learn that the point here is that God instructed Moses in many fine points of Torah, as well as to what the exegeses that the rabbis in generations to come would articulate and the advances to be introduced by scribes. What are they going to advance? The mitzvah surrounding the reading of the *Megilla*.

The next Mishna is extremely short. Everyone (including women!) are eligible to read the *Megilla*, with exceptions for the deaf, the insane, and those who have not yet reached an age when they can be taught to recite the *Megilla*. R. Yehuda demurs on the last case and states that a minor may read the *Megilla*. The first case is a recitation by a deaf person: have those who hear his (or her) reading fulfilled the mitzvah, or must they hear it again? First of all, the Gemara wants to know who offered this teaching. Rav Matna pipes up that it was R.Yose; in tractate *Berachot* (15a), we find it sanctioned for one who reads the *Shema* but didn't hear the words has nonetheless satisfied the requirements of the mitzvah, but R. Yose disagrees and requires a repetition. Same holds for the recitation of the *Megilla*. The Gemara suggests that to rule in this manner would mean that R. Yose was the Tanna of the Mishna, but there's no proof of that. Perhaps it was R. Yehuda who rules that it's better if the *Megilla* is read by a hearing person, but if a deaf person does read then it's effective, and the *mitzvah* has been fulfilled.

The Gemara isn't buying this. The list of ineligible "readers" also included an insane person and a minor, who are excused from performing any of the mitzvot, and even after the fact, so clearly the same must hold for the deaf. This refutation is also overruled, for why should placement in this list mean that the latter two categories dominate the first one? Maybe the Mishna really does accord with R. Yehuda.

So, Gemara now tries another tack to disprove that the Tanna was R. Yehuda. The last statement of the Mishna has R. Yehuda qualifying a minor as reader, so how could he possibly have authored the first part outlawing a minor as his work? Maybe, just maybe, R. Yehuda did argue both parts and sees two kinds of minors. The type which bans minors from reading refers to young people who have not attained an age to receive proper training in recitation of the text; minors who have reached that age, however, can surely be asked to recite, and this is the kind of minor whom R. Yehuda sanctions as legitimate.

The Gemara is still unhappy with R. Yehuda as Tanna of the Mishna. It claims that the comparability of ruling a recitation of the *Shema* by someone who cannot hear is acceptable after the fact. But, it does not tell us that R. Yehuda would not have accepted this. A *baraita* is raised at this point from which we learn that a person who is deaf but is capable of speech is permitted to separate *teruma* (the first portion of a crop that is set aside to be given to the *kohanim*, at which point it becomes sacred and can only be consumed by a member of the priestly class) even initially. This despite the fact that he cannot hear his own spoken blessings delivered as he executes the mitzvah. This can't be R. Yehuda's ruling, because in the case of reciting the *Shema*, he only accepted it as the fulfillment of the mitzvah after the fact (not initially). By the same token, it cannot be the view of R. Yose who claimed that even after the fact the mitzvah of the *Shema* has not been fulfilled; he could hardly rule differently regarding *teruma*.

What about another take on R. Yehuda's view on reciting the *Shema*? The Gemara raises another *baraita* to complicate matters further. Recitation of grace after meals (*birkat hamazon*) must be spoken out loud, but if one merely says it to himself (perhaps, while moving his lips), this is not preferred but acceptable. Whose position does this *baraita* reflect? Can't be either R. Yehuda or R. Yose. R. Yehuda would, logically, sanction positively an initial recitation, but that's out here; and R. Yose would not accept even an after-the-fact recitation, so can't be him either.

20a

Now, the Gemara offers something of a resolution. The *baraita* about *teruma* accords with R. Yehuda; and inasmuch as this *baraita* allows a deaf person to separate *teruma*, then the *baraita* accepting a recitation of *birkat hamazon* that was not heard must accord with the view of his teacher. What was his teacher's ruling? R. Yehuda (in the name of R. Elazar ben Azarya) claims that a reciter of the *Shema* must also hear it; after all, the verse is all about "hearing." The analysis reveals that it is preferable to hear, but if not heard, the mitzvah is fulfilled after the fact. R. Meir has a somewhat different understanding. Based on *Deuteronomy* 6.6, he claims that if the reader concentrates closely on the words as he speaks, then (being that he is deaf) not actually hearing does not disqualify the mitzvah. This is all very confusing,

At the tail end of the Mishna, R. Yehuda states that a minor can recite the *Megilla*. The Gemara takes this up by relating a *baraita* in which R. Yehuda himself tells of his experience as a minor reciting the text of the *Megilla* before R. Tarfon and the elders of the city of Lod. This is his substantiation, but they retort that backing for this ruling cannot be based on the experiences of a minor. All right, then, the Gemara points to another *baraita* in which

R. Yehuda ha-Nasi makes the same claim about reading the text before R. Yehuda when still a minor, and he too is turned down flat, only this time it's because he is citing as the authority for his ruling (R. Yehuda) the very man who allows this as fulfillment of the mitzvah. The two rejections together offer a major thumbs-down to R. Yehuda's view.

The Talmud moves on to a new Mishna now. Several rituals are listed as prohibited from taking place before sunrise: reading the *Megilla*, circumcision, purification by submersion if a ritual bath, and sprinkling with purifying waters following contact with a corpse. By the same token, a *zava* watching for menstrual discharge (see *daf* 8b) is also prohibited from submersion in a *mikve* before sunrise. If you do any of these things following a single ray of the new sun, the mitzvah is fulfilled.

How do we know this about launching a reading of the *Megilla*? Verse 9.28, which has been used a fair number of times thus far, refers to "these days" that are to be commemorated as the Purim holiday: "day" and not night. Now, R. Yehoshua ben Levi argued that one must recite the *Megilla* at night and repeat it by daytime; does this ruling contradict his view? No, the Mishna's articulation of the daytime requirement is referring to the second reading—and this practice is still the standard.

What about circumcisions? *Leviticus* 12.3 states that it must transpire on the eighth "day"—no differing views here. *Mikve* submersion and sprinkling? The Gemara only cites a verse for the latter (*Numbers* 19.19), again referring to "day," and submersion in a *mikve* by virtue of comparability with sprinkling is covered as well.

The last case of our Mishna concerning a woman observing herself for discharges might seem the most complex, but the Gemara uses a term to dismiss all doubts: *peshita* ([It's] obvious!). The terms in question is "counting a day for a day," meaning a clean day following one on which she experiences a discharge. The ritual is to count seven days without discharge before immersion, but in any event we're talking about "days."

20b

So, in all such situations, the mitzvah is fulfilled if carried out after dawn's early light. We've established that it has to be daytime, but what constitutes "daytime"? Is it the sun's rays? Rava takes us all the way back to *Genesis* 1.5, where we learn that God saw the light he had created and called it "day." The materialization of light (as dawn emerges) is what is meant here, according to the Gemara. Perhaps, though, this isn't the best use of that verse, for the same verse has God calling the darkness "night." Does that mean that the first indications of darkness constitute nighttime?

The Gemara tries another tack. R. Zeira cites a passage from *Nehemiah* (4.15) which speaks of work from dawn's first light until stars appear in the sky. At that point, night takes over. The Gemara equates the workday with these astronomical occurrences and thus the start of day and night are established.

The final Mishna of this chapter is considerably longer. It begins, still on the theme of "day," by noting that the mitzvah of reading the *Megilla* can take place at any time during the day. The same is true for an assortment of other rituals: recitation of the *Hallel* prayer, blowing the *shofar* (ram's horn used on certain holidays), taking out the *lulav* (palm branch used as part of the Sukkot festival), the Mussaf (additional) prayer, the confessional recitation over the bulls to be sacrificed (by the High Priest and the Sanhedrin for a serious communal error), the confessional recitation accompanying *maaser* (tithing) on certain days of the year, the confessional recitation offered by the High Priest on Yom Kippur over the bull to be sacrificed and over the goat dispatched to Azazel, the *semicha* or "leaning on" (the animal) performed by one who brings a personal animal sacrifice, slaughtering sacrifices, waving of portions of a sacrifice performed by the priest, carrying the vessel with the meal offering before the Altar, carrying out the *kemitza* ritual to be burnt on the Altar, gentle slaughtering of a bird offering in which the priest cuts through the back of the bird's neck with his (sharpened) fingernail, receiving blood offerings, sprinkling blood of sacrificial offerings, presenting the *sotah* (see glossary) with the bitter waters she must drink, *egla arufa* or decapitation of the calf (the ritual performed when a corpse who has clearly been murdered, no murderer found, and the elders of the nearest city decapitate a calf), and the purification ritual of a *metsora*.

Meanwhile, nighttime mitzvot can be carried out at any time during the night: reaping the *omer* (meal offering brought on Nisan 16) and burning of certain sacrificial fats and limbs of animal offerings. The overall ruling is stated in a straightforward manner: Any mitzvah designation for the daytime can be carried out at any point during day, and any mitzvah designated for nighttime may be carried out at any point during the night.

As is its usual wont, the Gemara proceeds to provide scriptural support for carrying out each of the daytime mitzvot at any time during the day. For the reading of the *Megilla*, it hauls out the tried and true verse 9.28, as we noted above. For *Hallel* it cites *Psalms* 113.3 (which is part of the *Hallel* blessing) which notes "from sunrise to sunset," we praise "God's name," although R. Yose prefers *Psalms* 118.24 which notes that "this is the day God has made." What about the *lulav*? Here, the Gemara points to *Leviticus* 23.40 which refers to "the first day" one is to take the palm branch. Blowing the *shofar*? *Numbers* 29.1 mentions "a day for blowing [the *shofar*]." And, the sacrifices offered at *mussaf*? *Leviticus* 23.37 mentions an offering brought each and every "day," which the rabbis identified with *mussaf*. How about the bulls confession? This time we are presented with a *gezera shava* lining up the word "atone" from *Leviticus* 4.20 and 16.11 (which concerns the offering on Yom Kippur); and "atonement" is carried out during the daytime, as we know from *Leviticus* 16.30.

The Gemara invokes *Deuteronomy* 26.13 about separating *maaser*, and shortly after it (verse 26.16) the daytime is cited as a commandment from God. Leaning and slaughtering certain sacrifices are both cited in *Leviticus* (3.8 and 19.6), and because the two are juxtaposed and the latter contains "on the day" in it, both are proven to be approved anytime during the day. The waving ritual is simple; *Leviticus* 23.12 says: "On the day of your waving the *omer*." Carrying the meal offering near the Altar? This one is a little less straightforward. This mitzvah coming right after waving suggests a comparison of sorts, and while *Numbers* 5.25 mentions both, the daytime allowance comes from waving. The delicate execution of a bird offering, the *kemitza* and its burning on the Altar, and the sprinkling of collected blood from sacrifices are justified on the basis of *Leviticus* 7.38 which involves a general commandment to perform certain rituals.

We come now to *sotah*, whose daytime performance is sanctioned by a *gezera shava*: "Torah" (*Numbers* 5.30) refers to the duties incumbent on the priests vis-à-vis the *sotah*; and "Torah" (*Deuteronomy* 17.11) refers to teachings and judgment from scripture.

21a

As judgment is a daytime practice, so too must be the drinking of the bitter waters by the *sotah*. Regarding the beheading of a calf, the Gemara lines up the word "atone" from *Deuteronomy* (21.8) where this ritual is laid out with reference to daytime mentioned with the sacrificial service (see above). That only leaves cleansing a *metsora*, and *Leviticus* 14.2 explains the law for a *metsora* "on the day" he or she undergoes purification.

The latter section of the Mishna, much shorter, deals with rituals that may be carried out at any point during the nighttime. While offering the *omer* must be done during the day, reaping it is to be carried out at night, according to a derivation in another tractate of the Talmud, *Menachot* (66a).[1] And, finally, *Leviticus* 6.2 decrees that the ritual of burning fats and limbs may be performed "all night until morning."

The overall ruling which recapitulates the day and night allowances seems little more than an explanatory exclamation point, and the Gemara wants to know what it adds. The phrase used to introduce this statement, *ze haklal* 'this is the general rule,' usually indicates that, yes, it is a general rule and, yes, the text has introduced a number of cases which fit the rule, but there are also other similar cases not mentioned. So, now it adds one more for the day side of the general rule, involving bringing the weekly show breads with the two spoons of frankincense which the priests bring to the Temple when they also remove the old. This one is contested (see *Menachot* 99b),[2] and explication will take us down an unnecessary rabbit hole. How about the nighttime rituals? Here, it cites consumption of the Pascal lamb on Passover, which a *baraita* notes follows *Exodus* 12.8 to a T: "and they shall eat the meat on that night." R. Elazar ben Azarya disagrees and provides a *gezera shava* with *Exodus* 12.12 which also has the phrase "on that night" (*balayla haze*) in which God tells Moses he will be killing the firstborn of the Egyptians at midnight, meaning it can't be at any time of the night. No definitive ruling ensues, as Chapter Two comes to a close.

Notes

1. See my *Grains of Truth*, pp. 215–16.
2. Ibid., pp. 335–36.

Chapter 3

Rules for Reading the *Megilla* and the Torah

21a (cont'd)

We begin with a ruling that the actual reading of the *Megilla*, in private or in synagogue, may be performed standing or sitting. If one person alone or two people simultaneously read the *Megilla* before a congregation in synagogue, all have fulfilled the mitzvah. Usually when two people speak at the same time, even if they are saying exactly the same thing, it can be confusing as to what is being said, but the mitzvah is fulfilled nonetheless (more on this to come). If the local custom is to say a blessing after the recitation of the *Megilla*, we do so; if not, no need. However, and this is not in the Mishna, the blessings before reading are compulsory everywhere.

The Mishna now segues to discuss how many people are called to read from the Torah on different days and at different times, and what additional readings are part of services on those occasions. Three people are called to read Torah in shul on Monday, Thursday, and the afternoon of Shabbat, although in reality it is a reader who performs the actual reading on behalf of the three people called in most synagogues. The Mishna makes clear that these numbers are fixed; also, on these occasions, unlike at Shabbat morning services, no reading from the Prophets is added. A blessing before and after the reading is required by the persons called to the Torah. At the beginning of each month (Rosh Chodesh) and the intermediate days of longer festivals, four people are called to the Torah, and this number (4) is non-negotiable; also no passages from the Prophets are read on these occasions. Blessings are recited before and after these Torah readings. A general rule follows: non-full-fledged holidays which still demand a *mussaf* service (Rosh Chodesh and intermediate days for longer festivals) require four people called to the Torah. On certain holidays (to be described) five people are called to the Torah, and on Yom

Kippur the number is six. On Shabbat, as is well known, seven are called. And, these numbers are also not up for debate. And, on these occasions, we conclude with a reading from one of the Prophets. During the week, to add the Prophets to the service may be wearying, but on Shabbat and full-fledged holidays that is not the case. And, finally, each Torah portion read must have a blessing before and after.

The rest of this chapter will explain all of these many rulings and have little to do with reading the *Megilla*. Contrary to the sitting option when reading the *Megilla*, a *baraita* teaches right off the bat that one must stand when reading Torah in shul. What source does the Gemara cite? R. Abbahu refers us to *Deuteronomy* 5.28 in which God instructs Moses to stand with him, as He teaches him Torah. Now, R. Abbahu knows full well that such anthropomorphisms are not to be taken literally; so, it is a figurative use of such language as regards God, but Moses (and the rest of those who follow) actually are to stand. The thing about anthropomorphisms is that, while we are strictly taught in this instance not to think that God actually stands, inappropriateness notwithstanding, the image lingers. R. Abbahu has a related teaching added here: using the same Torah verse, he rules that once mustn't sit on a couch while teaching Torah to a student seated on the ground. Both need be at the same level, either on the ground or on a couch. At this point a macho *baraita* is introduced by the sages to note that from Moses' time until that of Rabban Gamliel, all Torah learning was done standing, but thereafter a certain weakness set in, and people began learning Torah while seated. The Gemara cites a Mishna from tractate *Sotah* (49a) which states explicitly that, following the death of Rabban Gamliel, the Torah's glory came to a standstill, because people lacked the ability to stand while studying it and to offer it proper rectitude.

Moses' posture on Mt. Sinai is briefly brought up here, as it seems we may have a contradiction in Torah regarding it. *Deuteronomy* 9.9 and 10.10 have conflicting verses: the former records him saying that he "sat on the mount," while the latter states he "stood on the mount." Rav explains that Moses stood while studying Torah with God, but when he reviewed on his own what God had taught him, he would sit. R. Chanina has another take: Moses wasn't standing and he wasn't sitting; he was bowing, which may be understood as either posture, and it thus was so recorded in two different ways. R. Yochanan has yet another view: when verse 9.9 referred to Moses's "sitting," it was just a way of saying that he didn't move from one spot. He cites a verse from *Deuteronomy* (1.46) to point out that "sitting" there, too, can mean something like camped out at, but in fact Moses stood when studying Torah on Sinai. Lastly, Rava has an odd position: Moses studied the easy parts in the Torah while standing and the harder parts while seated, apparently because it was considered easier to concentrate on those tougher passages while seated.

The Gemara now turns to the Mishna's statement about fulfilling the mitzvah of *Megilla*, whether one person read or two people did simultaneously. What's the source to substantiate this?

21b

The Gemara starts by clarifying that, while this dual reading may work for the *Megilla*, it decidedly does not for reading Torah. This requires a little more exposition, because in the era of the Mishna it was often the case that the Torah would be read in Hebrew and then "translated" into the lingua franca of the era, Aramaic. The "translator" was known as a *meturgeman*, which like the word "interpreter" in English had a broad range of meaning. The *baraita* explaining this notes that two people may not translate simultaneously, which should indicate that two people ought not read Torah at the same time either, as the latter is more important than the former. Readings from the Prophets, by contrast, allow for one reciter and two translators; but, there cannot be two reciters and two translators. As for *Hallel* and the *Megilla*, no limit to the number of readers and translators—actually, the *baraita* says "even ten" can read. What makes *Hallel* and the *Megilla* different? The Gemara says these readings are cherished favorites by congregants, perhaps because they are chanted relatively infrequently, and therefore the listening is more intense.

The Mishna then noted that, if the practice in a given congregation is to offer a blessing after the *Megilla* reading, it must be followed. Abaye iterates that we're only talking about a blessing after the reading; the blessing before is required. Rav Yehuda (in the name of Shmuel) states that a blessing is always said before performance of a mitzvah. Now, what blessing is recited before recitation of the *Megilla*? The answer is unusual. On one occasion Rav Sheshet from Katrazya preceded Rav Ashi when reading the *Megilla*, and he delivered three blessings which the Gemara records with a mnemonic, *mem-nun-chet*: over reading the *Megilla*, a blessing for the miracle as well as the *shehecheyanu*, respectively. How about after? It's praise for God who "exacts vengeance for Israel" against our enemies. Rava goes for something a little less bellicose: praise for God's saving the Jewish people from annihilation. Rav Pappa proposes combining the two blessings, inasmuch as God did both.

We turn now to the numbers of people called to the Torah on different occasions. First, three people are called on Monday, Thursday, and Shabbat afternoons. Where, asks the Gemara, does this number come from? Rav Assi claims that they correspond to the three parts of the Tanakh: Torah, Prophets, and Writings. Rava has another idea: they correspond to Kohanim, Levites, and Israelites, the three bodies of the Jewish people. On the subject of numbers, the Gemara cites a *baraita* referred to by R. Shimi to the effect that no fewer than ten verses should be read in shul. Why ten? R. Yehoshua ben Levi says that they correspond to the ten men always available (see *daf* 5a) in synagogue; Rav Yosef suggests correlation with the Ten Commandments, and R. Levi points to the ten times that David employed the word *haleluya* (praise God) in *Psalms*. R. Yochanan says it's the ten statements by God ("and God said") which brought the world into existence. The Gemara retorts that there are only nine of these, but actually the first words of *Genesis* ("In the beginning") constitute an effective utterance which ushered in the world.

So, if we have three readers, how do we divide up the minimal ten verses to be read? Rava's plan is to have reader one recite four verses, reader two four verses, and reader three four verses. Yes, this comes to twelve. The idea embedded but not explicit is that, ordinarily, the division would be a combination of 3–3–4, with the reader of that extra verse earning special praise. So, Rava's idea is to have everyone read four. Different rabbis now present arguments as to why having one of the three readers deserve special praise is preferable.

The next piece of the Mishna firmly states that the number of those called to read is fixed. It apparently was once the case that the first one so called recited the opening blessing, and the last one so called recited the blessing after. That practice was at some point in time abandoned, because those who arrive late in synagogue might be confused when there, if they only, for example, see the middle person called and he fails to offer a blessing before his portion is recited. So, thereafter, everyone called to the Torah recites a blessing before and another after the reading.

Moving along to the ruling that four are called on Rosh Chodesh and the intermediate days of lengthy holidays. Ulla bar Rav asks Rava how the passage to be read is divided among the four. Ulla bar Rav goes on to explain the possible issue here. The Rosh Chodesh reading (*Numbers* 28.1–15) is comprised of three paragraphs with eight, two, and five verses, respectively. There is a rule that a given reader cannot finish his reading with less than three verses unread in the paragraph. If the first two readers each read three, that will leave two verses in paragraph one, which won't do. If the first two readers each read four verses, that leaves a total of seven verses, but how to divide them for the third and fourth readers? The third reader could read both verses of paragraph two and the first one of paragraph three, but

22a

this won't work either, because there is another rule that you're not supposed to stop reading less than three verses into a new paragraph. If reader three then reads through the third verse of paragraph three, that means that only two verses will be left which violates the previous rule.

Rava has a response. He acknowledges that his solution is not directly about Rosh Chodesh, but the approach just might work. His case concerns a Sunday Torah reading in two batches, *Genesis* 1.1–5 and 1.6–8, performed by the weekly group selected to lead the offering of communal sacrifices at the Temple. So, he suggests two people read the first set of five verses and one person read the second set of three. The latter makes perfect sense, but how are two people going to read the five verses of the former? A Mishna (actually the next Mishna in this tractate) dictates that no reader should read less than three verses; how can two readers divide five verses so that each gets no fewer than three? Rav has a very simple solution: reader one reads three, and reader two simply rereads the last verse of reader one and then the subsequent two verses. Shmuel suggests we can even split the third verse in half, so that each reader gets 2.5 verses.

This Rav-Shmuel disagreement now becomes the topic for analysis. Why was Rav not persuaded by Shmuel's two-and-one-half solution? Well, if a verse was good and whole enough for Moses, it's good enough for him and its wholeness should be preserved. There's another question, because R. Chanina (Chananya?) Kara had tried to divide verses when teaching children Torah, and he was allowed but only for youngsters. How could Shmuel so cavalierly suggested doing that for adults? The Gemara agrees that Torah is hard, and dividing it for purposes of elementary education is the only exception in this regard. Shmuel would assert that these weekly groups also required verse-splitting, inasmuch as he also believed Rav's plan for rereading a verse impossible. What is Shmuel's problem with Rav's idea? Again, there is a worry about people entering late or leaving services early; they will either see reader one read three verses or reader two start with verse three and conclude that reader one only read two verses. Either way they may feel that there is something rotten in the state of Israel. This concern with people wandering in late or leaving early is curious.

A new *baraita* at this point contests both of these answers, but the case it outlines is only, at best, tangentially related to the specific issue at hand. R. Tanchum (in the name of R. Yehoshua ben Levi) reiterates two operative principles here: one must read three verses from a new paragraph of scripture; and one may not abandon a paragraph with less than three verses remaining. The Gemara now asks if the second of these principles actually encapsulates the first. It demonstrates that it can't, because the latter restriction is the more stringent. The analysis now segues to the issue of latecomers, early leavers, and what each would hear and assume. How do we deal with these two perennial groups and make the division of verses read legitimate? Now, the Gemara offers a simple resolution. Those who arrive late, in the middle of the Torah reading, and observe a new reader pick up at a point which might indicate that the previous reader (whom they did not see or hear) only read one or two verses will turn and whisper to fellow congregants: what's up with this? They will then learn that the earlier reader read from the previous paragraph and that all is fine. The congregant who leaves early does not have this option, but the Gemara lets it go.

So, Rabba son of Rava asks Rav Yosef what the final *halacha* is in such a case. The reply is that the second reader (of three) rereads a verse, and thus both principles are kept intact.

Back to the rulings in the Mishna at hand, and here we are addressing those non-full-fledged (or semi-) holidays which also require *mussaf* sacrifices. The Gemara asks: How about public fast days—how many are called to the Torah to read? The question is elaborated a bit: inasmuch as there are no *mussaf* sacrifices on a fast day, shouldn't it be three readers (not four)? Yet, inasmuch as there is a special prayer (*aneinu*, lit. 'answer us') intoned by the congregational cantor on fast days, perhaps it should be four readers. First answer: public fast days are not listed in the Mishna, so not four but three. This is much too easy a response, and the Gemara dispenses with it almost as fast as it raises it. The Gemara tries another tack, this time via an actual case. One day Rav was visiting the city of Babylon on a fast day. He was called to the Torah to read, offered a blessing, read his portion, and when he finished, he did not offer a concluding blessing. The Gemara reasons that, inasmuch as he was neither a *Kohen* nor a *Levi*, Rav had to have read the third (Israelite) portion, but why no final blessing? Clearly, he was not the final reader, and thus a fourth reader would follow him to the Torah.

The Gemara, though, promptly rules this solution out, for Rav might have read the *Kohen*'s portion, despite not being a member of priestly caste. This is something Rav Huna (also not a *Kohen*) regularly did, given the high regard as a Torah scholar he enjoyed in his day. Rav would have enjoyed the same in his own day. The Gemara doesn't like the comparison of Rav and Rav Huna. The latter was more highly appreciated than the great *Kohanim* in the Land of Israel, while Rav usually deferred to Shmuel who also resided at the time in Babylonia. In response, the Gemara says that actually Shmuel deferred to Rav, while Rav always honored his regular disputant when he was present. Otherwise, Rav accepted his own pre-eminence in the region.

The Gemara reiterates that Rav must have read the *Kohen*'s first portion. If you still cling to the notion that he read the third portion, why did he recite an opening blessing when the Mishna makes clear that only the first reader does that? But, this "proof" is also quickly dismissed, because by the time this case transpired, the law was that every reader was responsible for both a fore and after blessing. So, he could still have been the third reader. But, if he was the third reader and this followed the new law regarding blessings, then why did he not offer a concluding blessing? Everything is different when Rav was the centerpiece of the discussion, and the rules aren't always so rigorously the case.

22b

So, the Gemara goes another route with a *baraita* stating that, on days when people lose time from work because they're held longer in shul—like public fasts and the Ninth of Av—the rule is that three are called to the Torah to read; that way, there's no loss of work time as there would be on holidays like Rosh Hashana or the intermediate days of longer festivals (when four are called to read), and the expectation is that no one is engaging in regular work. The Gemara actually approves and says this is a definitive proof: three readers on public fast days. And, then it offers a refutation, because, as Rav Ashi states, the Mishna rules that a non-full-fledged holiday with an additional *mussaf* sacrifice or *aneinu* prayer gets four readers. Shouldn't that ruling also cover public fast days and the Ninth of Av? The Gemara at this point must be dizzy from spinning back and forth, and it now dispenses with Rav Ashi's point by arguing as follows according to a *baraita*. If the Ninth of Av falls on a Monday or Thursday, three people are called to the Torah, and the third one reads and then continues reading with a passage from the Prophets. If it comes on a Tuesday or Wednesday, one person is called to read, and he also reads from the Prophets. R. Yose has another idea: in all such cases, three are called to read with the third one also reading from the Prophets. In the understanding of both the *baraita* and R. Yose, then, only three read on the Ninth of Av, contrary to Rav Ashi who claimed the number was four. One problem with discarding Rav Ashi's inference here is that "general rule" in the Mishna should include public fast days and the Ninth of Av. Nope, it answers itself once again, "general rule" here only includes specifically what the Mishna stated, not fast days. Yet, those specifically included are Rosh Chodesh and intermediate festival days—and those are explicitly days on which *four* people are called.

The Gemara's final word on this digression is interesting (and deserves a new paragraph). By "general rule," it claims, the Mishna was offering a mnemonic and is not meant to extend its ruling to other days on which four people should be called to read Torah. It wants us to differentiate between a full-fledged holiday and those semi-holidays, like the first and last days of Passover vs. the intermediate days. The general rule, then, is that when we have something additional to do, it requires one more person to be called. Consequently, Rosh Chodesh and intermediate days of longer festivals have required *mussaf* sacrifices, and as a result four readers; on holidays when it is prohibited to do the proscribed work, that additional obligation moves the number up to five readers; on Yom Kippur, when the violation of labor restrictions is more stringent and there is a fast, six readers are called; on Shabbat, violations of labor proscriptions mean death by stoning: seven readers.

We recounted a story just above about Rav on a fast day in Babylon; in it he was called to the Torah, recited a before blessing, read his portion, and then did not recite a post-blessing. We didn't mention that Rav also failed to perform the *tachanun* prayer which required falling to the floor, "on one's face." Why was that? We now learn that the floor was stone, and a *baraita* invokes *Leviticus* 26.1 against prostrating on stone ground "in your land." The three words in quotation marks (only one in Hebrew) imply one's own home, but on the stone floor of the Temple it is perfectly fine to fall down. Ulla adds that what the Torah bans here applies only to prostrating on stone.

So, suppose there was a stone floor in the synagogue at which Rav attended services. Was it just Rav or did all members of the congregation also have to desist from prostrating? No, there was only a stone slab at Rav's feet and nowhere else in that shul. Well, then, why didn't Rav move a few feet where everyone else was and fall on his face? He didn't want to bother anyone, because they would have had to rise in respect as he walked by them. Don't like that resolution, how about: maybe the whole synagogue had a stone floor, and Rav actually did prostrate with his limbs extended (unlike others present); this would match another of Ulla's admonitions that the Torah doesn't ban all types of abasement, just with limbs extended. So, why didn't he fall on his face—what's with the extended limbs? The Gemara again comes to his defense: Rav ordinarily recited *tachanun* in this fashion. Or, maybe Rav didn't actually recite *tachanun*, because, as R. Elazar claimed, as a Torah celebrity, he would not have been allowed. The Gemara cites *Joshua* 7.10 in which God instructs Joshua to get up from his prostrating stance, an indication that Joshua was too important a personage to perform such abasement.

We turn now to a *baraita* which defines various sorts of prostration. First, there is *kida* which refers to bowing down on one's face; a verse from *I Kings* (1.31) depicts Bathsheba performing this one. Then, there's *keria* which refers to getting down on one's knees; another verse for *I Kings* (8.54) describes it. The third is *hishtachavaa* which is a full-fledged prostration with limbs extended; this one is referred to in *Genesis* (37.10) where Jacob famously scolds Joseph for bragging about his fairly transparent dream.

For some reason, we learn, Levi was offering a demonstration of the *kida* for R. Yehuda ha-Nasi, and he went lame from it; it's actually a complicated bow and requires considerable strength and balance. R. Elazar doubts that Levi's lameness came from bowing but was probably a consequence of grumbling in a heavenly direction. The Gemara again goes for a compromise answer and says both caused his lameness.

Back to the issue of famous people not being permitted to fall to their faces when reciting *tachanun*. Rav Chiyya bar Avin recalls seeing both Abaye

23a

and Rava leaning to the side when praying *tachanun*. This would mean that two such major Torah eminences wouldn't fall on their faces but would lean sideways—presumably on stone floors. The practice in most synagogues nowadays is to lean one's head on the forearm usually balanced against the back of the pew in front of them, and all people irrespective of fame or notoriety may do this.

The Mishna went on to note that on full holidays five people are called to the Torah, and on Yom Kippur the number is raised to six. Who would have been behind this Mishnaic ruling? The Gemara starts by ruling out R. Yishmael and R. Akiva. Why? R. Yishmael took the admonition against increasing or decreasing the number of those called to the Torah seriously, so the increase of five and six, as the Mishna teaches, would have conflicted with his thinking; R. Akiva argues that five are to be called on holidays, seven on Yom Kippur, and six on Shabbat, with the proviso that we can decrease but not increase the numbers, but in any event offering numbers different from the Mishna.

Discounting R. Yishmael and R. Akiva doesn't get us much further in identifying the source of the Mishna. Rava suggests the source to be a Tanna of the school of R. Yishmael, citing a *baraita* taught there that coincides precisely with the Mishna, but this would (needless to say) conflict with the *baraita* just cited in which R.Yishmael has a different view. The Gemara "resolves" this dilemma by averring that the different rulings reflect the views of two different Tanna's version of their teacher's teaching.

The Gemara now interject a somewhat related *baraita* in an effort to uncover its source. On regular holidays, we come later to shul and are anxious to leave promptly, presumably because we have preparations to attend to for the festival meal and get home to enjoy time with friends and family. The *baraita* continues that on Yom Kippur, it's the opposite: we arrive early and leave later, presumably because it's a fast day and thus no need for food preparation. And, on Shabbat we come early and leave early, allowing ourselves more time to end the day of rest. Question: Who rules that we should stay longer in shul on Yom Kippur than on Shabbat? Perhaps, it's R. Akiva who suggests an extra (seventh) person called to the Torah on Yom Kippur. But, maybe it's R. Yishmael who notes that, while fewer are called to read, the service tends to be longer on Yom Kippur, meaning that congregants remain longer.

Why do we assign the numbers of readers specified in the Mishna to those particular days: three for Monday-Thursday-Shabbat afternoon, five for full-fledged holidays, seven for Shabbat? R. Yitzchak bar Nachamani and R. Shimon ben Pazi disagree here, although we don't know who takes which side. One of them says it reflects the 3–5–7 pattern of verses in the *birkat hakohanim* (*Numbers* 6.24–26); the other claims it parallels the "three guards at the threshold" (*II Kings* 25.18), the "five who saw the king's face" (*II Kings* 25.19), and the "seven who saw the king's face" (*Megilla* 1.14). Rav Yosef then cites a *baraita* which exactly replicates the latter view. In an almost comical exchange, Abaye asks Rav Yosef why he didn't offer this explanation until now; the latter replies that he didn't know it was so urgently needed, and did he fail to respond to a question regarding it?

Someone named Yaakov asks Rav Yehuda now to explain what six readers on Yom Kippur signify. Rav Yehuda claims that they match the six persons standing on either side of Ezra (*Nehemiah* 8.4) when he read Torah in the Temple: all twelve are named here. There seem to be seven on his left, but it turns out the last two names are the same person ("Zechariah Meshullam"); we know this because all the other names are separated by "and."

Now we get an interesting *baraita* concerning who may be called to read Torah, and it refers to seven, so it must be referring to Shabbat. Those seven, though, can include minors (boys under thirteen) and even women. Before one begins to outline in his or her head a long tradition of shuttering women and preventing them from full participation in the religious life, the same *baraita* insists that women ought not read Torah in shul out of consideration for the dignity of the congregation. The idea is that, if a woman is called to the Torah, that means the men not called must be of lower capacity at reading Torah. It is not mentioned why, but it is easy to see the sociology behind this ruling. Interesting that the entire *baraita* is cited, conflict included, especially the initial allowance which would be anathema in Orthodox congregations everywhere. And, what happens if the "dignity of the congregation" allows for egalitarian considerations?

The Gemara now turns to the *maftir* (the final person called to read a portion of Torah and then a passage from the Prophets). The question is if the *maftir* counts as one of the seven on Shabbat. Rav Huna and R. Yirmeya bar Abba have opposing views here, with one saying he is counted and one saying not, though we don't know which of them says what. The one who says he counts supports his view by noting that the *maftir* does in fact read some Torah. The other follows a ruling from Ulla who ruled that the *maftir* is called to read from the Prophets; he reads Torah out of respect for Torah, for if he were to only read from the Prophets, it might appear to equate it with Torah. His primary job is to read from Prophets, so he doesn't count in the number prescribed for Torah readings.

This view, of course, cannot go unopposed. The Gemara cites a *baraita* that claims that anyone reading the selection from the Prophets mustn't read fewer than twenty-one verses which matches the minimum number of verses of Torah to be read (seven readers, minimum of three verses each). So, if the *maftir* also reads his requisite three verses of Torah, then the *baraita* should have required twenty-four verses from the Prophets. The answer given is simply that the *maftir* reads Torah out of respect for it,

23b

so there's no reason to overdo it with the Prophets. Nowadays, what the *maftir* reads from Torah repeats the last part of what the seventh reader read, making this discussion academic, but that must not have been the case when this topic was debated.

Rava points out that the mandated twenty-one verses doesn't work for Shabbat "Tsav" which only has seventeen ("Tsav" from Jeremiah 7.21–8.3), and we nonetheless read it then. The Gemara replies that verse 8.3 ends discussion of the topic at hand and thus legitimizes concluding the reading there. The Gemara doesn't buy it, because lots of topics end earlier than twenty-one verses in many readings from the Prophets. Rav Shmuel bar Abba claims numerous times to have read a mere ten verses before R. Yochanan who then ordered him to stop. So, there's nothing special about twenty-one. Final word on this Mishna is that we must differentiate places where a *meturgeman* is used to translate and even explain verses. If there is no need for one, then the rule of twenty-one remains intact, but if a translator is needed then it is thought too tiresome for the congregation to listen to that many verses and explications, so the reader may stop before twenty-one.

A new Mishna takes up more rulings about Torah and Prophet readings as well as the necessity of a quorum (*minyan*) of ten adult males present when such readings are performed. It starts with a long list of prayers and ritual practices which demand the presence of a *minyan*. So, without a *minyan*: no dividing the *Shema*, no repetition of the *Shemone Esrei* prayer, no priestly blessing, no public Torah reading from a scroll, no reading by the *maftir* from the Prophets, none of the rituals of standing and sitting associated with funeral processions, no recitation of the mourners' blessing and consolation of mourners, no wedding blessings, and no mention of God's name in the traditional invitation to join in grace after meals. When consecrated land is to be redeemed, its appraisal requires the presence of nine men and one *Kohen*; similarly, if one wishes to offer the Temple treasury an amount of money equal to his personal value on the slave market, the process requires ten men (one of them a *Kohen*). The Gemara will clarify some of these practices.

The Gemara begins by asking outright: how do we know all of this? In the name of R. Yochanan, R. Chiyya bar Abba begins the explication with a verse from *Leviticus* (22.32) from which he derives that all matters of holiness (such as dividing the *Shema* and repetition of the *Shemone Esrei*) require a *minyan*. But, there's nothing in the verse about ten men. R. Chiyya, however, derives this understanding from a *gezera shava* involving the word "among" (*toch*). The word appears in the *Leviticus* verse and also in *Numbers* 16.21. Neither of these verses, however, clear up how we get to ten men being required, so the Gemara offers another *gezera shava*, this time involving the word "congregation" (*eda*); it matches the latter verse of the previous *gezera shava* with *Numbers* 14.27. These two verses concern two troubling cases that faced the Israelites in the wilderness, the rebellion of Korach and the spies sent to investigate the Land. Both of these cases involves ten men, and via the "among" matching, the first verse of which includes mention of "sanctified among the Children of Israel," we come to regard any time in which God's sanctification is invoked requires a *minyan*. And, this is the origin of the custom in all Jewish communities to this day of requiring a quorum of ten adult men (or, among egalitarian congregations, of ten adults irrespective of gender) for public prayer. You read it here.

As for the standing and sitting ritual practices, the leader of the funeral procession refers to the people following along as "dear ones" (*yekarim*). That necessitates a *minyan*. How about the mourners' and wedding blessings? First, though, it asks what the mourners' blessing is (this is not *kaddish*); it is defined as the blessing offered to the mourners (who are not counted in the *minyan*) after a funeral at the first meal to comfort them. The wedding blessing, albeit a happier occasion, also requires ten men, but the groom counts.

Why do we need a *minyan* to mention the name of God in an invitation to say grace after meals? The one who does the inviting begins with "Let us bless our God." Fewer than ten men would be disrespectful, inasmuch as God's sanctification is being invoked.

The land and human appraisal are slightly different: still need ten men, but one must be of the priestly caste. What in scripture makes this so? The reasoning in this instance is so convoluted that I am somewhat embarrassed to even try to describe it. I shall leave this to the keener students of Talmudic hermeneutics. There is in fact a pushback (also convoluted), and the Gemara resigns and refrains further defense of this view. I suppose we're fortunate that redeeming consecrated property for appraisal is not nearly as current an issue as it may once have been. As for assessing one's own value on the slave market as a measure of how much one wishes to donate to the Temple, the Gemara likens this to the previous assessment (of land), but I think I shall leave this sticky issue as it is.

On to a new Mishna and more about practices of reading from the Torah. As discussed above, each reader must read a minimum of three verses. If there is a *meturgeman* present, the reader must read one verse at a time so the translator can convey each verse to the congregation.

24a

For the Prophets, the reader can read three verses at a time for the translator, the reasoning being that, inasmuch as no laws are drawn from the Prophets, the fear of serious misunderstandings in translation are considerably reduced. If, though, three verses from the Prophets constitute three paragraphs, we go one at a time with translation interspersed. When reading passages from the Prophets, it's OK to skip sections, but this is not acceptable when reading Torah. How much in the Prophets is it acceptable to skip? It depends on how long it takes to roll the scroll on which the text is transcribed to get to a new section; if the translator finishes translating and scrolling continues, that is not appropriate.

The Gemara starts with the three-verse requirement for each reader and asks what they match. Rav Assi offers the simplest explanation, the three components of Tanakh: Torah, Prophets, and Writings. This is followed by the complicating factor of a translator present and the need to read those verses one by one, though readings from the Prophets can go three at a time, unless they are comprised of three individual paragraphs which must be read separately. The Gemara gives an example of three sequential verses (beginning with *Isaiah* 52.3) which require being fed to the translator individually.

The next passage in the Mishna concerns skipping through sections in the Prophets (OK) and in Torah (not OK). The Gemara notes (citing a Mishna from tractate *Yoma* 68b) that the High Priest reads consecutively from two sections in *Leviticus* which jumps over a large numbers of verses. Is this not skipping in Torah reading? Abaye to the rescue: the Mishna at hand is referring to the ban on skipping when the *meturgeman* has to wait for the reader to find his new place. The ban does not affect situations in which no waiting is required. The two passages read by the High Priest on Yom Kippur are from Leviticus, so it takes no time to speak of to roll the Torah scroll. Well, maybe not to the rescue, as the Gemara is quick to point out a fairly obvious point overlooked by Abaye: the Mishna allowed this sort of skipping when reading from the Prophets, but the Mishna is quite clear about disallowing such with Torah.

Perhaps Abaye didn't understand the question, so he tries again to resolve the dilemma of the two contrary Mishnayot: the Mishna in *Yoma* allows for skipping when the reading covers a single topic, but here our Mishna bans skipping when two distinct topics are in play. A *baraita* is promptly brought out to support this understanding of the situation. A further *baraita* is also marshalled here to modify things slightly: skipping when reading from the Prophets cannot jump from one book to another (probably, too confusing), although in the volume of the Twelve Prophets (all relatively short) skipping between books is permitted; also, no skipping from the end of any one book all the way to its beginning.

Time for another (meaty) Mishna. The person honored to be *maftir* (reading, actually rereading, the last verses of the weekly portion of Torah and then a selection from the Prophets) is the one who "divides the *Shema*"; he stands in front of the ark and repeats the *Shemone Esrei*; if he happens to be a *Kohen*, he intones the *birkat hakohanim* with hands raised; if he has yet to reach thirteen years of age, meaning he can't do any of these things yet, his father or teacher performs the duties on his behalf. Now, a minor may read Torah before a congregation and translate, as needed, but the aforecited tasks (as already noted) are off limits to him. If his legs are uncovered, he is allowed to "divide the *Shema*" and serve as translator, but reading from the Torah, standing before the ark, and lifting his hands are all off limits; same holds for a blind man, although R. Yehuda restricts someone who was born blind. Some of the foregoing will surely need elucidation.

The Gemara begins by asking why the *maftir* is afforded such honors. Rav Pappa gives the bare-bones answer: to honor him for agreeing to read the passage from the Prophets and presumably for continuing to lead prayers. Rabba bar Shimi answers the same question by saying that the *maftir* might otherwise come (figurative speaking) to blows with the prayer leader; this is rather confusing, but it seems to have something to do with compensation. If the *maftir* is still a minor, the Mishna delegates the other duties to his father or teacher. Perhaps, the Gemara suggests, we grant the prayer-leading honors to the *maftir* because he might otherwise clash with the regular prayer leader; but would a minor in this situation argue that he, too, should be so honored? No, no, retorts the Gemara, for minors have no expectation of being afforded such honors. In such a situation, the honors go to the father or teacher.

24b

Now, we have two possible contenders to launch a dispute. Maybe that's what the text was getting at.

Why is it, asks the Gemara at this point, that one who has uncovered legs is not to read from the Torah. Ulla bar Rav asks Abaye specifically if such a semi-clad minor may read Torah before the congregation. The unspoken piece here is that no adult may do this, as *Deuteronomy* 23.15 makes absolutely clear, but a minor is not as yet required to observe the mitzvot. Abaye's reply is a little off-color, but the gist is that this would insult the honor of the congregation and is thus off limits.

The Mishna ruled that a blind man is allowed to "divide the Shema," but R. Yehuda ruled it out for someone blind from birth. The rabbis queried R. Yehuda about this, saying that many have expostulated on the *Merkava* (the chariot of Ezekiel's vision), although they can't say they actually saw it. In other words, sighted people don't have a monopoly on imagination. R. Yehuda makes a distinction: explicating the *Merkava* reflects internal thoughts upon which one can focus one's mind and thus "know" it without having "seen" it; the case at hand involves a blind man leading prayers for the congregation, and thus the latter gains advantage from the objects of prayer, but not the blind man, which apparently rules him out. The rabbis don't see it this way. R. Yose explains, via a verse (*Deuteronomy* 28.29) he claims to have struggled with for years, that a blind man can receive advantage even as he aids those who are sighted.

Another Mishna now: The priestly blessing (*birkat hakohanim*) may not be invoked with hands raised by a *Kohen* who has blemished hands. The blemishes are likely a distraction and an eyesore; nowadays, the *kohanim* cover head and hands with a prayer shawl. R. Yehuda adds that a *kohen* whose hands are stained with dyer's (bluish) woad is also forbidden from raising his hands to offer a blessing on the congregation—again, a distraction.

The Gemara begins with a *baraita* which extends to his face and feet, in addition to his hands, the sites of blemishes that bar a *kohen* from performing this ritual. What kinds of blemishes are we referring to here? R. Yehoshua ben Levi explains: spotted hands, and a *baraita* corroborates this aspect of the ban; also hands that bend forward or sideways are also disqualifying.

While we're on the subject of disqualifications, the Gemara now launches into a series of them. First up, Rav Assi offers a fascinating one: a *kohen* from Haifa or Beit Shean can't perform this blessing because they pronounce the Hebrew letters *alef* and *ayin* backwards and might confuse the prayer. Nowadays, very few can distinguish these two letters (both are usually silent), a wonderful datum for historical linguists. The Gemara inserts here a play on letters with potentially unhappy consequences, but this one does not appear to be philologically significant.

Rav Huna states that a *kohen* whose eyes are full of tears is disqualified, probably because congregants will gaze at him and be distracted. The Gemara mentions a case of someone who fit this bill in Rav Huna's locale and still was allowed to perform *birkat hakohanim*. Rav Huna said nothing. That was a *kohen* who was well known in the area, and a *baraita* is cited at this point which makes this explicit.

R. Yochanan avers that a *kohen* blind in one eye can't lead the priestly blessing, again because curious congregants will gawk; if he has no apparent indication of the eye's inability to see, then he's good to go. A similar case to the one above is raised about a local man blind in one eye who led this prayer—no one complained. Reason: also, he was well known in the area. And, again, a *baraita* delivers just this ruling here.

The Gemara to this Mishna returns to the main teaching: a *kohen* with stained hands may not bless the congregation, but a *baraita* is now raised so that we know that, if the majority of men in the city in which such a *kohen* lives are dyers and are thus familiar with stained hands, our original man is not outlawed from delivering the *birkat hakohanim*. Same reason: he (or at least his discoloring) is a familiar sight to congregants and will not induce gawking.

The new Mishna is structured a little differently. If someone says that he refuses to stand before the ark to lead the congregation in prayer if he is wearing colored clothing, then he is barred from doing so even in white garments. If he says that he will not do this with sandals on his feet, then he is barred from doing so even barefoot. If someone somehow makes his head *tefillin* round (its normal shape is a cube), he exposes himself to danger, and there is no advantage in doing this (not a mitzvah). If he sets the head *tefillin* down on his forehead (rather than just above the hairline) or the arm *tefillin* in the palm of his hand (rather than on his bicep), this is sacrilegious. These two placements reflect practices of the Sadducees and hence are deemed heretical. If someone were to plate his *tefillin* in gold, or if he set the arm one on his shirtsleeve and not on his skin directly, this follows the ideas of people straying from mainstream Jewish practice.

The Gemara dispenses with the first two pieces of the Mishna, the two professed refusals, due to colored clothing and sandals, to lead prayers, as the result of someone possibly influenced by heretical thoughts. If there is such a possibility, he should be ushered off the *bima* (lectern on which the Torah is read). The ruling about round *tefillin* squares with a *baraita* teaching that the prescribed shape of the *tefillin* is a law received by Moses at Mt. Sinai. Rava corroborates this as well. Rav Pappa offers a thought that effectively claims that the Mishna and the *baraita* cannot lead to the disqualification of a rounded *tefillin*. This is left uncontested, although I don't believe there are any round *tefillin* out there.

Our *daf* comes to a close as it barely has time to introduce the first word (only one of the next Mishna). If one were to say

25a

(and this is odd): "May good men bless You," this is heretical. Apparently, even evil people bless God; and, as there are odiferous elements used in the production of the Temple's incense, so too must evil sorts be included among the Israelites. This is contrasted with the next ruling: If one were to say that God's compassion reaches the "bird's nest" or thank God for His good deeds or simply "we offer thanks, we offer thanks," such a person is to be silenced. By way of explanation, in *Deuteronomy* (22.6) we are instructed to shoo the mother bird away before we extract her babies from the nest; one is not to slaughter a mother animal and her offspring on the same day. We also silence anyone who explains straightforward Torah dictates against proscribed sexual unions in an oblique manner. The worst is that we not only silence but also condemn anyone who reads *Leviticus* 18.21 (about prohibiting handing your children to priests of Molech) and claims it means not to impregnate an Aramean woman.

The Gemara accepts silencing for saying "we offer thanks" twice, because it might seem as though one is separately thanking two deities; and for thanking God solely for good deeds He provides, because we must accept and praise God even for bad things. But, what's up with the bird's nest? This was apparently debated by two commentators in the Land of Israel: R. Yose bar Avin and R. Yose bar Zevida. One of them states that the silencing here is a result of praising God's compassion as it might arouse envy as though God has elevated a bird above other members of the animal kingdom; the other makes an important distinction, for the mitzvot are not acts of compassion but, literally, commandments, not debatable issues.

The Gemara now offers a learning-by-example. A man was to lead services before Rabba, and he mentioned in his prayers the praise of God for the bird's nest business, and that God should show his faithful followers the same compassion. Rabba lauded this, but Abaye wondered aloud to Rabba if this behavior, in fact, warrants silencing, as indicated by our Mishna. Rabba then effectively pats Abaye on the back for catching this lesson which was presented to him, apparently, as an intellectual test.

The Gemara follows with a similar case. Another man proceeds to lead prayers before R. Chanina and offers a series of laudatory adjectives for God. Several of these the man added on his own, meaning they were not part of the standard *Shemone Esrei* liturgy. Three of his praises, R. Chanina tells him, are sanctioned by the Torah and fixed by the Men of the Great Assembly, but by adding those extra compliments, it is as though God needs them. Analogy: a man has countless gold pieces, and people commend him for possessing silver.

And, as long as the Gemara is introducing a ruling from R. Chanina, it offers another. To him is attributed the famous line: All is in the hands of Heaven except for the fear of Heaven. This is supported by a line from *Deuteronomy* (10.12) that what God expects only from the Jewish people is that they fear Him. If that's all, isn't that just one little thing, the Gemara asks.

Actually, we are told, it is a small thing, though the analogy here is confusing and does not bear repeating.

R. Zeira now suggests that, like the person who states "we offer thanks" twice and is therefore silenced, the same should be true of one who says "*Shema*" twice. This is questioned but not ferociously. Yes, reading the *Shema* twice in succession is detestable but not enough to silence such a miscreant. What was R. Zeira getting at? What he was criticizing was someone who repeats the *Shema* verse by verse—worthy of silencing. The *baraita* was speaking about someone who repeated it word-by-word: real bad but not rising to the need for silencing. Rav Pappa makes a reasonable suggestion to Rava: maybe said person didn't sufficiently concentrate the first time he read the *Shema* and now he is doing just that. Rava replies sardonically: Are we supposed to behave as if we're Heaven's pal? Failure to concentrate? Smack him good! Then, he'll learn to concentrate.

The Mishna rather harshly forbad oblique explications of the Torah's injunctions against illicit sexual unions. Rav Yosef claims this refers to anyone who dribbles around parental incest but does not confront it directly. As for the Mishna's ban on delivering children to priests of Molech and the siring a child with an Aramean woman, the Gemara cites a *baraita* coming from the academy of R. Yishmael: the verse refers to a Jew who engages in a sexual union with a Cuthite woman, which then results in a child she can devote to idolatry.

New Mishna time, the final one of this chapter. Mentioned above several times was the practice at the time the Talmud was compiled of reading the Torah and Prophets and then having a *meturgeman* translate into Aramaic, the *lingua franca* of Jews at the time. This new Mishna addresses certain passages that were not translated as well as certain portions of the Prophets that were never included in those ascribed to the *maftir* at all—the problem is that they are either unflattering to our ancestors or might be so be conceived by congregations.

We start by noting that the story of Reuben (*Genesis* 35.22) is read but not translated; this recounts how he had sex with Bilhah, his father's concubine. The rabbis explain any apparent indecency away, so that people able to understand the Hebrew will probably understand the nuance here, but not the masses. Yet, the story of Tamar (*Genesis* 38) is both read and translated; this is surprising, but the Gemara will explain. Similarly, the first story of the Golden Calf (*Exodus* 32.1–20), very uncomplimentary to our distant ancestors, is read and translated (see below). Yet, what the Mishna refers to as the "second" part of the story (*Exodus* 32.22–24) is read but not translated: here, Aaron describes to his brother how the Calf in question emerged from the fire, and the unwashed masses might understand this as if the Calf was a sentient entity unto itself; so yes in Hebrew but not in a language the ignorant might understand. Two more passages read but not translated: the *birkat hakohanim* (*Numbers* 6.22–27) which we have discussed before and the story of David and Amnon (see *II Samuel* 13). Finally, the section on the *Merkava* from *Ezekiel* is not included in any readings from Prophets as part of the *maftir*, though R. Yehuda allows it. R. Eliezer bans chapter 16 of *Ezekiel* because it notes outrages committed there.

The Gemara starts with a mnemonic to distinguish scriptural passages that are: (a) read and translated; (b) read but not translated; and (c) neither read nor translated. Mnemonics of this sort appear frequently in the Talmud, harkening back to a time long before the invention of printing, of course, when the text was not written down but memorized. The mnemonic makes no sense in English, as it is comprised (usually) of the first Hebrew letter of the scriptural passage concerned. In any event, it starts right at the beginning, and we do, of course, read and translate the creation (*Genesis*). Why even ask such a silly question? The Gemara replies that maybe people will ask questions about what is above and below the world that God creates, or

25b

what came before and what might come after. Maybe by translating these early scriptural passages we are tempting fate. The Gemara just, basically, tells us to stop worrying. Further in *Genesis*, the story of Lot and his two daughters (19.31–36) is both read and translated. Isn't this obvious, the Gemara answers its own question. Well, whatever one may think of their behavior with their father (each conceived a child with their own father, based on the mistaken belief that the human race was otherwise at an end), the good name of the girls' uncle, Abraham, might be called into question. Nope, stop worrying.

What about the story of Tamar and Judah (*Genesis* 38), asks the same *baraita* which is basically running down a list of sexual behaviors that might certainly make one feel uncomfortable. Of course, we read and translate. But, mightn't Judah's honor be compromised. Nope, he confessed his bad judgment and behavior. All right, then, the first part of the Golden Calf story, which is actually mentioned in the Mishna is also read and translated—obviously. Isn't this story a huge embarrassment to virtually all Jews except Moses? This time we learn that translating this important passage will serve as an annual atonement, even inspiration toward repentance, for the people. The "curses and blessings" (*Leviticus* 26 and *Deuteronomy* 27) are both read and translated, of course, despite the depressing messages in the curses—the blessings are fine. Stop worrying.

There are warnings and punishments throughout the Torah, and we are to read and translate them. The problem here is that people might be driven to observe the mitzvot solely out of fear. The *baraita*: not to worry! What about the tale of Amnon and Tamar: read and translate; same for the story of Avshalom, despite his illicit relations with members of his father David's harem. Don't worry about the good name of David, father to Amnon and Avshalom, as the people can handle it.

Moving to a reading from the Prophets, we are to read and translate the story from *Judges* (chapter 19) of the concubine in Gina, despite a fear of embarrassing the tribe of Benjamin. What about the passage in *Ezekiel* (16.2) about the "abominations of Jerusalem"? Yes, read and translate. R. Eliezer wanted it banned as a *maftir*'s reading, but the *baraita* includes it here.

Now, on to portions of scripture that may be read in Hebrew but ought not be translated into Aramaic. It starts with another mnemonic. The first story to be treated in this fashion is the one mentioned in the Mishna about Reuben. We get here a fascinating story of R. Chanina ben Gamliel on a visit to Kabul. The cantor in synagogue was reading this passage from the Torah, and just before he mentioned Reuben's indiscretion, R. Chanina told the translator to skip rendering that verse for the congregation. He was applauded by the sages for his effort.

The second part of the Golden Calf tale (referring to *Exodus* 32.21–25) refers to Aaron's description of the incident to his brother. A *baraita* explains how R. Shimon ben Elazar used this to make the very case noted above. How about *birkat hakohanim*? The problem here is the mention (from *Numbers* 6.26) of God "lifting His face" to you, and this may convey the erroneous notion that God favors the Jewish people over others. The passage about David and Amnon? If the passage about Amnon and Tamar, as noted immediately above, is OK to read and translate, what's the problem here? Just the few words linking Amnon directly with David; earlier, we only mentioned Amnon.

There are other verses in the Torah that are written rather indecently, but we need to read them nicely. This can take some work. What does the *baraita* have in mind? It offers half a dozen examples, mostly single words or just letters which convey the intended meaning but without the coarser veneer of the literal text. Rav Nachman states in this connection that no mocking is allowed except for mocking idolatry. R. Yannai gives another example of a slight change of a reading in one word from a phrase in *Hosea* (10.5) to soften the language.

Rav Huna bar Manoach (in the name of Rav Acha son of Rav Ika) begins the conclusion of chapter 3 with an interesting and acceptable practice. A Jew is allowed to tell an idol-worshiper to take his idol and put it in his *shin tav*. Rashi explains that these two Hebrew letters spell *shet* which means one's rear end (*Isaiah* 20.4); this is undoubtedly behind the contemporary English expression: "shove it!" Rav Ashi claims that, if one's name is dragged through the mud, one may shame the culprit involved with *gimel shin*. There are several explanations for this combination of letters: none of them complimentary in the least. Ending on a positive note, praises for someone with a fine name are perfectly fine.

Chapter 4

Laws of the Synagogue and Torah Readings

25b (cont'd)

The first Mishna of the fourth and final chapter of this tractate turns initially to a discussion of the sanctity of the synagogue and the Torah scroll. When a holy object is sold by town residents or synagogue board members, the money received takes on the same level of sanctity as the object; it can then be used only to purchase an object of equal or great holiness. Again, in matters of holiness, we only raise but do not lower. What are these levels of sanctity? Suppose the residents of a town sell off the town square, then the only purchase that can be made with that money is a synagogue. So, if they sell a shul, the only purchase they can make is an ark. If they sell an ark, only Torah wrappings can be bought. And, if they go and sell Torah wrappings,

26a

the only purchase available to them is scriptural texts. Should they sell such books, then the only available purchase would be a Torah scroll itself. This is what one *can* buy.

If they were to sell a Torah scroll, buying books of scripture is out—based on the dictum of only raising, not lowering, in matter of holiness. Proceeds from selling books may not be used to buy Torah wrappings. Selling such wrappings cannot lead to the purchase of an ark, and selling an ark cannot lead to buying a synagogue. Finally, the sale of a synagogue cannot lead to buying a town square. If any money remains after the purchase of an item of greater holiness, that remainder must also be used for something of greater holiness.

The Gemara now launches into discussion of each of the rulings of this Mishna. First, the residents of a town sell their town square with the only purchase option from the proceeds being a synagogue. Rabba bar bar Chana (in R. Yochanan's name) argues that the idea of a town square enjoying a degree of holiness must be attributed to R. Menachem bar Yose, who often offered rulings anonymously. In fact, Rabba suggests, town squares have no inherent holiness, and proceeds from their sale can be used for anything desired. What might have been the basis for R. Menachem bar Yose's argument? Among other things, because on certain fast days the ark is carried out to the town square for the people to pray for rain. The response to this idea is that a town square is only made use of on such irregular occasions, not as a consistent matter of course.

Next, if a synagogue is sold, the Mishna ruled that only an ark can be bought. R. Shmuel bar Nachmani (in R. Yonatan's name) rules that this dictum applies only when selling a rural synagogue. If the shul is in a city, and people come to it from all over, the town folk have no right to sell it. Why? Because it belongs to the public at large, not just to those townies. Rav Ashi offers a specific case, a synagogue in the city of Mechasya, the town in which he lived. He makes the odd claim that, yes, the synagogue is in a city, and, yes, people do come there from outside the city, but they come to study with him. So, if he wanted to, he could put that synagogue on the market.

Further disputations with R. Shmuel bar Nachmani ensue. R. Yehuda tells of a synagogue of copper workers in Jerusalem, the directors of which sold it to R. Eliezer, and he then put it to personal use. The deal was seemingly kosher, despite the synagogue having lost its holiness. Obviously a city synagogue, and R. Shmuel would never have allowed it to be sold to R. Eliezer, but it happened nonetheless. The Gemara gives this incident a pass: it was a small shul built by and mostly for those copper workers themselves. Further contestation concerns whether or not synagogues in Jerusalem are impervious to *tsaraat* impurities (the walls of buildings, like people, can be), but it appears that R. Shmuel's ruling survives the challenge.

In the foregoing, the Tanna of the *baraita* argued that the reason Jerusalem was not so vulnerable to *tsaraat* was that the city, as home to the Temple in which all the tribes of Israel had rights, was not distributed among the tribes. R. Yehuda, on the contrary, argues that it was, which means that buildings in Jerusalem are vulnerable to *tsaraat* and its laws. So, inasmuch as the Temple grounds covered areas belonging to the tribes of Yehuda (Judah) and Binyamin (Benjamin), which parts of it fell to the tribe of Yehuda? And, for that matter, which fell to the tribe of Binyamin? The Gemara lays out the pieces apportioned to each, as well as some digressional data, but the bigger picture here is that this view sanctions the notion that Jerusalem was distributed when the land of Israel was.

The Tanna of the *baraita* takes the opposite position about Jerusalem and begins his rebuttal with a *baraita* indicating that renting houses in Jerusalem, primarily meaning renting rooms to pilgrims to the city at holiday times, was prohibited. Why? Because these are not theirs to offer, belonging as they do to all Israel; they must be available for free. R. Elazar bar Tsadok adds that one may not rent out beds in Jerusalem either. So, those who had beds or rooms on offer would be "paid" with hides of the animal offerings brought by the pilgrims. Abaye concludes this string by suggesting that proper etiquette would dictate that a pilgrim leave behind a jug and/or a hide for his host.

Rava now offers an idea to slightly alter the ruling about purchasing something of higher holiness. This applies in the case of the sale of a synagogue (or any property possessing holiness), of course, but only if the seven town leaders do so without the town residents present. If sold publicly, then they can even

26b

use the cash as beer money. The Gemara proceeds to offer an illustration of this emendation of the Mishna. Ravina owned some fields and the ruins of an old synagogue sat on one part of them, just rubble at this point. He asked Rav Ashi if the law allowed him to turn it into farmland, or would the former sanctity of the shul foreclose this possibility. Rav Ashi directed him to approach the seven leaders of the town and buy it before them and the public. Then, he could proceed to plant on it. This all seems a little odd, for if Ravina did indeed own the field on which the rubble sat, what would he have to "buy" from the town?

The Gemara turns to another story to illustrate the issue of synagogue holiness. Rami bar Abba was constructing a new synagogue to replace an old one. He first wanted to tear down the old one, take raw materials from it, and use them in building the new one. Before he launched into this, he was in the study chamber, thinking through a teaching of Rav Chisda, instructing us to first build the new one before bringing down the old. Rav Chisda was worried lest, after destroying the old synagogue, one might neglect to build a new one, leaving the people without a shul. Rami bar Abba, then, was clearly taking down the old to use to build the new one. Stymied, he went to Rav Pappa and laid out his case; Rav Pappa ruled against him. So, he went to Rav Huna who also ruled against him.

Referring to the ruling about synagogues, Rava notes that we can exchange it or sell it, as prescribed, but we may not rent it out or mortgage it. Why is that? Because by just renting or mortgaging, the synagogue remains in its state of holiness and would thus be a desecration. So, Rava continues, one can exchange or sell the bricks of a synagogue, but lending them is banned. This ruling applies only to old bricks that were once part of a shul that has since crumbled. He continues in this vein to demonstrate that only after bricks are used in the construction of a synagogue wall do they become part of the synagogue itself, including its sanctity.

Following in this line, how about a case in which someone gave the synagogue to the community as a gift? What happens to the sanctity of the synagogue? Rav Acha and Ravina take different sides over this issue. One of them deems secular use of the shul off limits, while the other allows it. The former notes that a gift is not an exchange, meaning that the synagogue's holiness remains intact. The latter argues that there had to have been some reciprocity in donating the shul, so whatever it was constitutes something comparable to a sale.

A parallel case: how do we deal with objects used in carrying out a mitzvah? Can we toss them, inasmuch as the item retains no vestige of holiness. Accessories to sacred objects, though, do indeed retain their holiness and must be secreted in a safe spot, never to be used for another purpose and never to be discarded. Mitzvah objects include: Succah, *lulav*, *shofar*, and the ritual fringe on garments (*tsitsit*). Accessories to sacred objects include: bags for carrying sacred texts, *tefillin*, *mezuzot*, cases for carrying Torah scrolls, and *tefillin* bags and their *tefillin* straps.

Rava has some ideas, actually five of them, on this front. He claims that he had thought the *bima* was an accessory of an accessory to a mitzvah, because the Torah is placed on a covering over the lectern, meaning that the lectern was available for non-sacred uses. But, then he observed a Torah being set right onto the lectern, meaning it was a direct accessory and hence off limits to secular tasks.

Rava had a similar first impression about the curtain lining the inside of an ark, because it appeared to be a second-degree accessory to the ark's purpose of storing a sacred Torah scroll. That would mean this curtain could be repurposed to any use, but he later observed it being folded in such a way that the Torah sits right on it; it thus retains all sanctity and cannot be used to any other end.

Rava states that if an ark, in which one stores a Torah, collapses, we may repurpose it to build a small ark—no lowering of sanctity involved. However, to use its raw materials to construct a lectern is prohibited, inasmuch as an ark possesses greater sanctity than a lectern.

Rava had also thought that a worn ark curtain might be repurposed as a coverlet for the Torah scroll itself, as the two items (curtain and Torah covering possess equal sanctity). However making a worn curtain into the coverlet for a single book of the Torah is out, as it lacks the level of holiness of the whole Torah.

Finally, Rava states that the bags used to carry individual books of the Torah and cases for entire Torah scrolls are both considered accessories to sacred objects and must thus be secreted. Obviously, states the Gemara, why even mention it? One might claim that such bags and cases are not meant to preserve the honor of the objects within but just to protect them, meaning that their function deemed them short of the inherent sanctity of the objects being housed within. Rava teaches otherwise.

The Gemara segues here to examine another, vaguely related teaching. A synagogue of Roman Jews had a doorway into a morgue, and there was a body there. *Kohanim* (who are prohibited from corpse impurity, *Leviticus* 21.1) wanted to come and pray at this shul and presented their dilemma before Rava. He suggested they carry the entire ark over and have it block the doorway into the morgue. Being made of wood, the ark could trap the impurity in the morgue, preventing its spread beyond, and at the same time not itself become impure. However, the ark was occasionally moved a bit when the Torah was taken out or replaced inside, and it had to remain immobile to be insusceptible to impurity. When faced with this predicament, Rava accepted that it would be impossible to impede the spread of impurity.

The Gemara now assesses how certain holy objects need to be dispensed with. Mar Zutra, from whom we have not heard as yet in this tractate, claims that wrappings of all sacred texts (including Torah scrolls) cease to be proper for their job when they become worn out. How do we conceal them? He suggests using them as shrouds for an unattended corpse. What about a Torah that has clearly seen better days? Rava opines that it may be hidden by burial next to a Torah scholar, even a scholar of the less penetrating aspects of Jewish law. Rav Acha bar Yaakov states that such a worn Torah needs to be put inside an earthenware vessel for burial—that will hinder rapid corrosion.

On the question of levels of sanctity, how does a synagogue compare with a Torah study hall? Rav Pappi (in Rava's name) avers that transforming a synagogue into a Torah study hall is allowable, but the reverse is not. Having cited Rava's ruling, Rav Pappa promptly states that he disagrees. Rav Acha

27a

provides a solution: Rav Pappi has got it right, as Rav Yehoshua ben Levi once stated that a synagogue may be transformed into a study hall, for the latter must have a higher degree of sanctity than the former.

Now, Bar Kappara cites a verse from *II Kings* (25.9), about the burning to the ground of all the houses of God, of the king, and of all Jerusalem by Nevuchadnetzar's general. He interprets the "house of God" to be the Temple, the "house of the king" to be the royal palace, and "all the houses of Jerusalem" to be (as seems transparent) all the "great houses" of the city. So,

R. Yochanan and R. Yehoshua ben Levi expound on the term "great houses," although we don't immediately know who holds which view. One says it points to places at which the Torah is greatly illumined, while the other says it means places at which prayer is greatly illumined. Both views have supporting opinions as well. Now, the Gemara identifies R. Yehoshua ben Levi as the one who voted for the Torah, as it was he who said that a synagogue can be converted into a study hall, the latter being the very place Torah is studied and illumined in and by the minds of the scholars there.

The Mishna went on to claim that proceeds from a sale of a Torah cannot be used to purchase scriptural texts, as the degree of sanctity would decrease in such an instance. This much is clear. But, what about using the proceeds to buy another a new Torah? The degree of sanctity may not increase, but it surely doesn't decrease. The Gemara will chew on this interesting case for a while. The Mishna is only explicit in the phrase cited immediately above: no selling a Torah to buy individual scriptural texts, because the latter are of a lower degree of holiness. That just might imply that buying another Torah is okay. This line of reasoning is rejected, as no inference in this case may be allowed.

So, the Gemara tries another tack. A *baraita* permits wrapping a scroll of the Torah in the wrapping of a single book of the Torah and single Torah books in wrapping from books of the Prophets or Writings, but not volumes of the Prophets or Writings in wrapping from volumes of the Torah, nor single volumes of Torah in wrapping of an entire Torah scroll. The implication is that, while the wrapping from single Torah volumes may be used for a Torah scroll, the Torah wrapping from one scroll to another may not. And, that, by extension, means buying a Torah with funds from the sale of another is out. This "proof" seems a little shaky; if wrapping from a Torah scroll may be used for single Torah volumes, one could just as easily infer Torah-to-Torah is okay. The Gemara thus concludes that the *baraita* proves nothing hard and fast.

The Gemara now makes a third attempt using yet another *baraita*. Placing a Torah scroll on another Torah scroll is permitted, just as placing a Torah on a scroll of a single book of Torah. Nothing sullied here. Single volumes of Torah can be set on top of books of the Prophets or Writings—again those of higher sanctity on top. But, the reverse is definitely out—no books of the Prophets or Writings can be set atop books of the Torah, nor for that matter may individual books of Torah be placed atop an entire Torah scroll. So, if one Torah scroll can be set on top of another, they are of equal sanctity, and the sale-and-purchase option should be doable. Again, this is outright rejected because the logic just isn't there: the *baraita*'s ruling does not lead there. There may be an issue of room to work in that placing one Torah on top of another is legit. When a Torah scroll is rolled up, individual pages of parchment sit on top of other pages. There's actually no way to avoid this. Individual pages are not hierarchically differentiated, as objects of equal holiness may sit atop one another, but that does not lead to carte blanche on our sale-to-purchase issue.

Another approach ensues. Rabba bar bar Chana (in the name of R. Yochanan who taught this in the name of Rabban Shimon ben Gamliel) states that one is not allowed to buy an old Torah with proceeds from a new one. So, this Torah-for-Torah sale and purchase is banned. The Gemara rejects this proof as well. His ruling was based on the fear that, after selling their Torah, the people would not immediately buy another and their money would be squandered. What if we can assure that the issue of neglect will be obviated? Or, is it a question of Torahs being exceptions to the rules? R. Yochanan (in R. Meir's name) states an interesting (and, at first glance, seeming contradictory) ruling: it is permitted to sell a Torah only so as to learn Torah, which means to support oneself studying Torah, or so as to get married. The sanctity of a Torah itself is then analogous to studying it. The Gemara actually rejects this line by stating that Torah study can (and should) lead to performing mitzvot, meaning that it transcends the sanctity of a Torah scroll. Where, you might justifiably ask, did that enter the equation. The Gemara cites *Isaiah* 45.18 which is very nice but not terribly related to our context.

After all this back-and-forth, the Gemara comes to the conclusion that selling one Torah to buy another is not to be sanctioned. It does add another related *baraita* as a precaution. Aside from the two ends noted above—to support oneself studying Torah or to get married—there is no good reason to sell a Torah, even if it has seemingly used up its usefulness (if that is conceivable). Rabban Shimon ben Gamliel adds an even harsher addendum: even if one has scarcely enough to eat and sold his Torah scroll, or sold his young daughter into indentured servitude as a maid to acquire food, that money will never lead to any good end.

The last phrase of the Mishna at hand refers to leftover monies from the sale of a holy object which may be used solely for something of a higher degree of holiness. Rava notes that this refers to the use of money left over after buying something of higher holiness with funds from a sale. One exception would be the collection of monies from the public to buy something, the purchase was made, and some money remained. That cash is available for any purpose.

Abaye disagrees, citing a *baraita* about this verse's piece of the Mishna. He claims that, only if the party holding the extra money after the sale had not stated they would be using it for non-sacred ends, must it go for the purpose of a sacred object. If they had so stated, it's available—even to hire a *duchsusya* (see below). His argument is straightforward. Failure to state clearly their intentions to use the leftover money for non-sacred ends means it can't be so used. The Gemara isn't buying this and claims that the *baraita* raised by Abaye actually substantiates Rava's point.

Abaye asks a reciter of *baraitot* before Rav Sheshet a question: Did Rav Sheshet ever explain what a *duchsusya* is? Answer: a town courier, someone who took messages from town to town on a horse (H. *sus*). Abaye draws a lesson of an ethical nature from this exchange. If a young scholar hears a word he doesn't understand, he should ask someone who often finds himself among rabbis, such as at an academy. Such men will surely know.

As he did a moment ago, R. Yochanan now states a ruling in R. Meir's name. In the event of one group of people traveling to another town, they may be taxed for charitable ends by the town visited. When they are ready to go home, they should get the same amount back to support the poor in their own town. The Gemara cites a *baraita* at this point which totally supports this ruling and then adds the case of a single person traveling to another town. He may be taxed and should pay up, but the money stays in the visited town as charity for the poor. Yet, the Gemara limits this teaching with a case. Rav Huna announced a fast in his town due to a drought. Visitors from another town came to join him in the fast, and the local administrators collected a charity tax from them. They complied and when they set off to return home, they asked Rav Huna if the tax money might now be returned to them, which they stated would be used for the poor of their own town. Rav Huna cited a *baraita* that specified, if

27b

there was a scholar of the town involved in charity work in the community, then the funds should remain in the locality where it was collected. Thus, no, it stays with me and my town was his reply.

A new Mishna is upon us. R. Meir rules here that residents of a town are not allowed to sell a public synagogue, meaning one used by at least ten persons, to an individual for any purpose, because it would spell diminution of its sanctity. The rabbis respond that, if this be so, then large city selling a synagogue to a small one should also be disallowed, because that would seem to also involve a lowering of its holiness.

R. Meir replies to the rabbis with a seemingly obvious retort. As regards switching ownership of a synagogue from a big to a small town—the synagogue was sacred then as it is now. But, when the synagogue building's ownership goes from the public to an individual, the latter's employment of the shul (with no *minyan* now) has considerably less holiness, meaning a decline has transpired. What's the rabbis' response? They see a clear lessening of sanctity when a shul moves from large-to small-city ownership. They cite a verse from *Proverbs* (14.28) to stress the more the better, and R. Meir should accept this decrease.

The Talmud leaves this one unresolved at this point, and turns to a new Mishna, again launched by R. Meir. He rules that, the residents of a town are permitted to sell their synagogue solely with the proviso that, should they ever want it back, it has to be returned. The rabbis state that the same people may sell their synagogue unreservedly unless the purchasers will turn it into one of the following four institutions: a bathhouse, a tannery, a *mikve*, or a laundry. R. Yehuda adds that, if they sell it to be made into a courtyard, the purchaser is at liberty to use it as he wishes (presumably, even if he chooses to turn it into one of the four items just noted).

R. Meir's initial ruling here seems rather open-ended. Should the proviso be used to nullify the sale and the money be returned to the purchasers, we may have a problem. The latter will have been using the shul for a period of time, and such "free" use of the synagogue constitutes interest which is clearly banned by the Torah. R. Yochanan offers a unique interpretation; namely, when the sale of the synagogue was transacted, there was an allowable use for it, and that would mean that no interest was involved. Thus, R. Meir's teaching was made in accordance with the view of R. Yehuda, and R. Yehuda (in the language of the Gemara) sanctions "interest" in only one aspect. Needless to say, this argument sparks debate, and after some back-and-forth, this matter, too, remains unresolved.

The Gemara now takes up the allowance of a synagogue's sale except in four instances. The first opinion cited here might seem a bit strange. R. Yehuda (in Shmuel's name) claims that one may urinate within a range of four paces of a place of prayer. When R. Yosef suggests this teaching is old hat, R. Yehuda fires back from our Mishna that the synagogue may be sold to be turned into a courtyard, and the purchaser may then do with it as he wishes—even turn it into a urinal, contrary to the rabbis. The rabbis distinguish between a synagogue and a place of prayer which does not have eternal sanctity (as a synagogue does). Thus, they agree with R. Yosef that Shmuel's teaching is redundant.

At this point a reciter of *baraitot* rehearses one before Rav Nachman: after praying, one moves four paces away from this place of prayer before urinating, and (vice versa) one who has urinated ought move four paces from that place before commencing prayer. Rav Nachman accepts the latter half of this formula, but he has issues with the former half. If he has to move four paces away from any place of prayer, then most every pathway in his city of Nehardea would be off limits to urinating. He suggests emending the *baraita* to waiting the time it takes to walk four paces rather than that he should walk four paces away from the place of prayer. The Gemara asks what the point of waiting is. Rav Ashi claims that, while walking those four paces, one is still finishing his prayer, and prayer while peeing constitutes a desecration.

The Gemara now launches into a long digression discussing certain habits of four Tannaim. First up is R. Zakkai who is asked by his students how it is that he has reached a venerable old age. He replies that he never urinated within four paces of a site of prayer (despite Rav Nachman's demonstration that it would have been okay to do so), he never used a nickname for a colleague, and he never forgot to recite the prayer over the wine on Shabbat—in each case, he chose a more stringent custom for himself. R. Zakkai expands a bit on this last practice. Once when he had no money to buy wine over which he would have enunciated the accompanying prayer, his elderly mother sold her veil to buy the wine. A *baraita* notes that when she passed away, she left her beloved son 300 barrels of wine, and when R. Zakkai died he left his own children 3,000 barrel of wine.

In a digression to the digression, the Gemara recounts how dedicated to the prayer over wine that Rav Huna was. Once when he was with Rav, he was wearing a belt made of grass. Rather surprised, to say the least, Rav asked him what he was up to. He explained that he had been forced to pawn his belt for money to buy wine. Rav was duly impressed and blessed him that in due time—forget grass—he'd have clothing made of silk. Years later, he found himself in a much better monetary place.

The second Tanna, R. Elazar ben Shamua, was similarly asked by his students how it was that he had been blessed with long life. He replied that, his whole life long, he had never used a synagogue as a shortcut (which the next Mishna will outlaw), he never stepped over the heads of his students sitting on the ground around him, and as a *kohen* he never forgot to invoke a prayer before *birkat hakohanim*.

The third Tanna, R. Preida, was also asked this question by his students. His response: he was always the first person into the study hall,

28a

he always deferred to a *kohen* when a group offered the prayer of grace after a meal, and he never ate the meat of an animal whose parts that were supposed to go to a *kohen* had not been. The Gemara stays momentarily on R. Preida's refusal to recite grace after meals when a *kohen* was present. R. Yochanan notes that any Torah scholar should lead this prayer and not defer to an ignorant *kohen*, and the Gemara confirms that R. Preida, in practice, only deferred to a *kohen* who was at least his equal in Torah wisdom.

The fourth Tanna, R. Nechunya ben Hakkana, is also asked this question by his students. He replies: he never gained any sense of righteousness from humiliating another person, he never allowed another's oath not be resolved before the day was over, and he was unstinting with his money. The first of these three claims is illustrated by a story involving Rav Huna. Rav Huna was walking along carrying a spade, when he bumped into Rav Chana bar Chanilai. The latter asked him if he might help out and carry the spade for him, but Rav Huna responded that, only if it was Rav Chana's practice in his town to carry equipment would he allow it, for otherwise it would appear to honor Rav Huna at Rav Chana's expense. As for the second explanation, R. Nechunya offered to explain his longevity, the Gemara relates that, like Mar Zutra, he would always say as he climbed into bed that he forgave everyone who had exasperated him that day. Regarding R. Nechunya's openness with his money, the Gemara tells of Job's practice of always offering an extra *peruta* (penny) to shopkeepers, presumably meaning he was a good tipper.

On another occasion, R. Nechunya responded differently to the same question, this time posed by none other than R. Akiva. Before their master can reply, R. Nechunya's servants smacked R. Akiva, as they thought he resented R. Nechunya for his old age and thus disrespected him. Undoubtedly not accustomed to such a reception, R. Akiva promptly climbed a palm tree to flee from these aggressive people. From his treetop perch, R. Akiva called down a question to R. Nechunya who, recognizing the erudition of this still quite young scholar, told his servants to back off. After he answered the erudite query for his guest, R. Akiva apparently climbed down. R. Nechunya now responded to the original question: he never accepted gifts, he never sought payback for offenses against him, and he was unstinting with his money.

We've already had the third item in this list of three explained, so the Gemara now proceeds to elucidate the first two. The refusal to receive gifts was just like R. Elazar who wouldn't accept gifts from the house of the president of the Sanhedrin. He never attended banquets when invited, citing *Proverbs* 15.27. R. Zeira also never allowed gifts into his home from the president of the Sanhedrin, but he did attend banquets to which he was invited, because the inviters were grateful for his being there. As for never seeking retribution, Rava notes that anyone of such caliber will have all his bad deeds removed at the time of final judgment and cites *Micah* 7.18.

Apparently, four Tannaim are insufficient for the Gemara, as it turns to another. R. Yehuda ha-Nasi asked R. Yehoshua ben Korcha this same question. Perhaps offended, he threw the question back and asked if R. Yehuda envied his length of years. No, of course not, he just wanted to know his teacher's Torah learning which had seemingly afforded him such a long life. That settled, R. Yehoshua replied: he never looked at an evil person's face. The Gemara cuts here to events that transpired several generations later which reveal teachings about looking into the faces of wicked people. A number of examples of the bad things that can happen by doing so are raised, focusing on Esau who takes the brunt of this string. Back to R. Yehuda ha-Nasi's encounter with R. Yehoshua ben Korcha, and as he was leaving he asked the elderly R. Yehoshua if he would bless him. Yes, he replied, may God grant you half as long a life as I have had. R. Yehuda ha-Nasi then wondered aloud why not ask for the entire span, this time clearly envying the older man's length of years. R. Yehoshua gives a cryptic, rhetorical response: Would you then have those who come after you mind the cattle? In other words, if you live a very long time, your descendants will never ascend to inherit your status as head of the Sanhedrin and will perforce remain ordinary folk forever.

One more great Tanna, R. Zeira, is asked the same query by his students. His reply: he never expressed anger in his own home, he never walked in front of a person of greater Torah wisdom than himself, he never contemplated Torah issues in dirty backstreets, he never walked even four paces without having a Torah thought or wearing his *tefillin*, he never slept in the study hall (neither overnight or even so much as a catnap), he never exhibited *schadenfreude* at the lapses of colleagues, he never used nicknames, and (some say) he never called colleagues by their "surnames" (did Jews have surnames in late antiquity?)

A new Mishna picks right up where the last one (*daf* 27b) left off. R. Yehuda rules that a synagogue that has become so decrepit that no one uses it any longer for prayer still holds onto its holiness. That means that one is not allowed to eulogize an ordinary person (meaning someone not a Torah scholar) there; no twisting ropes or spreading nets there (now that it's no longer a house of prayer, maybe someone thought these ordinary practices would be okay); no using its roof to dry fruit; and no cutting through it to save time. All the normal constraints of an operational shul remain intact. The Mishna invokes *Leviticus* (26.31) to equate even abandoned synagogues to sanctuaries, which thus means that the former remains sanctified. One last instruction: if grass starts growing in an old, decrepit synagogue, we are not to tear it up but must allow it to grow as a way to move people to sorrow.

The Gemara starts with a *baraita* that lays out what we are directed not to do in a synagogue: no easy-going humor, no eating or drinking,

28b

no prettifying (oneself), no wandering around, no using them in the summer to avoid hot weather or in rainy season to avoid the rain, and no small-scale eulogies for ordinary people. What we're allowed to do: read from Scripture, study Torah and Mishna, and offer public eulogies. R. Yehuda asks when this *baraita*'s ruling was issued, and the answer is while a synagogue was still in use. When not, they should be left as is—and let the grass grow, if it does within, for the very reason expressed in the Mishna. The Gemara seems puzzled by R. Yehuda, because it assumes the business about grass referred to a synagogue in use. A little more explanation clarifies the issue.

Rav Assi next opines that synagogues in Babylonia are constructed for general public use. No joking or amusement inside, though. He poses the question concerning what might be meant by this and responds that one mustn't carry on business within. Apparently, he really means business (not that sort), because any synagogue so misused will, he declares, become a morgue someday. Is it that bad, asks the Gemara. Rav Assi clarifies that he means unattended corpses, those for whom no relatives are known and thus for whom the community must take responsibility.

Now, the Gemara will take the *baraita* apart piece by piece. What did it mean by ruling out a synagogue as a place to prettify oneself? Rava said Torah scholars and their students actually may use a shul to this end. R. Yehoshua ben Levi called a shul a "home for Torah scholars," which would substantiate Rava's point. What about the injunction about using a synagogue to escape the heat or rain? Case in point: Ravina and Rav Ada bar Matna were together asking Rava a question. Just then it started to rain, so they went inside a synagogue. How did they explain themselves? They were engaged in a halachic conversation which requires clarity of mind. Rav Acha son of Rava asked a related question of Rav Ashi: How do you beckon someone out of shul in time of need? In a sliding scale of Torah knowledge, he should enter the synagogue and recite a halacha, a Mishna, etc., and if he knows none of these, he should either ask a child to recite whatever verse he studying.

The *baraita* also stated that a public eulogy may be given in a synagogue. The Gemara asks for an example. Rav Chisda and Rav Sheshet both indicate a eulogy in which the other attended would rise to that standard. Three further examples are offered as well—from Rafram, R. Zeira, and Reish Lakish. The Gemara segues into a discussion about the honor due a Torah scholar, alive or not. Many of the incidents in the Talmud involving Reish Lakish are difficult to understand, and that holds for one recounted here whose aim is to explicate the essence of honor and humility. In any event, learning Jewish law is always important, and that is where this string concludes.

The Gemara now turns to a discussion of joining a funeral procession and the honor thus accorded the deceased. It begins with a *baraita*.

29a

Two things are named as necessitating that one suspend one's study of Torah: participation in a funeral procession and attending one's daughter at her wedding. R. Yehuda is the prime figure behind this dictum. There is the qualification that, if the required number of persons are already present at a funeral procession, no suspending Torah study permitted. What is that number? Rav

Shmuel bar Inya (in Rav's name) claim it is 12,000 men and 6,000 with *shofars*; some explain that those 6,000 are part of the 12,000. Thus, minimum 12,000, maximum 18,000. Rav Sheshet heightens the hyperbole by offering a number of 600,000—the number that left Egypt at the time of the exodus and were present at the giving of the Torah in the desert shortly afterward. We are, of course, only speaking here of Torah scholars; for someone who hasn't studied Torah, one need not even suspend his studies.

The Gemara now cites a lengthy *baraita* taught by R. Shimon ben Yochai, concerning how the Shechina had always accompanied the Jewish people in their exile and will join them at the time of the ingathering of exiles. So, asks the Gemara, where is the Shechina in Babylonia? Abaye locates it in the synagogue in Hutzal and in the synagogue in Nehardea that had been destroyed and rebuilt (destroyed in Jerusalem and its materials brought to Nehardea and used to build this synagogue). We are immediately cautioned that the Shechina is not always present at both sites but moves back-and-forth. The Gemara concludes this string concerning the specialness of this synagogue with two stories of visitations from the Shechina witnessed by famed rabbis.

More on synagogues follows. A phrase from *Ezekiel* (11.16) about God as a "minor sanctuary" is cited, and like many in this text, it is not immediately clear what the meaning is. R. Yitzchak clears up that Ezekiel is referring to the Babylonian synagogues and study halls, and R. Elazar says it points to the home of Rav, his teacher. Continuing in the vein, the Gemara next has Rava cite *Psalms* (90.1) about God as an "abode"—he also points to this meaning of synagogues and study halls. Abaye tags on that this verse and *Psalms* 26.8 inspired him to both pray and study in synagogue. R. Elazar Hakapar offers a pronouncement via a *baraita*: with the coming of the Messiah, the synagogues and study halls of Babylonia will be built in the Land of Israel. This is followed by some confusing discussion of the role of anthropomorphized mountains in all this. This clearly requires some homiletical readings, and needless to say Mt. Sinai wins the day. The lesson is that haughtiness, even in mountains, is not a good trait.

The Mishna mentioned that we mustn't use synagogues as a shortcut. R. Abbahu moderates this ruling by noting that, if there was a previous pathway through the area now filled by a synagogue, one may use it as a shortcut. And, Rav Nachman bar Yitzchak adds that, if one went into a synagogue for a valid purpose, he may later use it to shorten his trip. R. Chelbo basically restates Rav Nachman's teaching, adding that you can enter a shul to pray and then leave by an exit that abbreviates the trip (citing *Ezekiel* 46.9).

The Gemara turns to the intriguing part of our Mishna about allowing grass to grow in an old synagogue as a means of moving people to sadness. A *baraita* qualifies this with a different message. No tearing up the grass to feed to animals, but one may tear it up and leave it right there. Thus, it is allowed to pull up grass in a decrepit synagogue. I imagine the sight of torn grass on the floor of a synagogue would be no less sad as growing grass.

The Gemara now segues to behavior in cemeteries. A *baraita* rules that there should be no frivolity, no grazing of one's flock, no water channels coming through, and no yanking up the grass there. If someone had a lapse and pulled up same grass, he must burn it immediately out of deference to those buried there. The Gemara asks how this last demand makes any sense—what deference is being shown by burning the grass? The reference to deference here goes with the start of the *baraita*: deference demands that one not act frivolously in a cemetery.

The attentive reader will have noticed that it has been quite a while since we were discussing anything to do with the *Megilla* (which is, after all, the name of this tractate). The new Mishna tangentially relates. Just as we read the *Scroll of Esther* on Purim, other pieces of Scripture are required reading on other occasions, and their content is the new Mishna topic. The *Megilla* is read in the middle of the month of Adar. That month is also a time for other special readings. If Rosh Chodesh (I Adar) coincides with Shabbat, we read (in addition to the regular weekly portion) *Exodus* 30.11–16 (*Shekalim*) concerning the half-*shekel* tax on all adult males. If Rosh Chodesh arrives on a weekday, this extra portion is added to the previous Shabbat reading; and they also interrupt the reading of the four portions (see below) on the next Shabbat. On the second Shabbat of Adar, we read *Deuteronomy* 25.17–19 (*Zachor*); on the third Shabbat we read *Numbers* 19.1–22 (*Para Aduma*); and on the fourth Shabbat we read *Exodus* 12.2. With the fifth Shabbat we return to the regular annual cycle of readings. Each holiday requires special Torah readings, not part of the annual cycle, which concern those holidays. We also have special readings for: Rosh Chodesh (other ones), Chanukka, Purim, fast days, watch days, and Yom Kippur.

The Gemara starts with a Mishna from another tractate of the Talmud which also notes that Adar 1 is when the court declares the half-*shekel* tax

29b

and the ban on *kilayim* (planting certain mixtures of vegetables and fruits). The latter ban makes perfect sense, as the beginning of Adar coincides with planting (actually, by then the planting season is over and sprouting should be apparent). But, why is it appropriate for the declaration of the half-*shekel* tax? A Torah verse mentions that a new month is a good time for buying a communal offering with monies collected from such a toll. So, the tax is assessed in Nisan and the *Shekalim* portion is read on Adar 1.

So, the call to pony up the half-*shekel* goes out some thirty days before the money is removed from the communal coffers to be used. Where did this period of thirty days come from? Not Rabban Shimon ben Gamliel for whom two weeks suffices, in a position regarding preparations for Passover. The Mishna elsewhere suggests by implication two weeks should suffice.

What is the actual *Shekalim* portion? Rav claims that it is *Numbers* 28.1–8, which details the daily burnt offering often referred to as "My offering, my food," while his perennial interlocutor Shmuel claims *Exodus* 30.11–16, which details the actual commandment to donate the half-*shekel* often referred to as "When you take count." The latter is actually called the *Shekalim* portion because of its content, but the former has no mention whatsoever of this tax. Defense of Rav follows the idea that the reason to assess and collect the tax is to fund the burnt offering, even if this connection is not explicit in the verses.

Coming to Rav's position are the arguments that his suggested portion does refer to the duty to bring public offerings, and by the same token Shmuel's suggested portion does mention offerings but not the ones for which the half-*shekel* is collected. Shmuel's stance is promptly reinforced, and then a back-and-forth with supporting arguments goes on for quite a while, involving among other items the added reading about Yehoyada from *II Kings* (12.1–17). This is actually the longest debate of this sort in tractate *Megilla*. The conclusion is where the Mishna began, and this round goes to Shmuel.

The Gemara now turns to Shmuel's itinerary for the readings for Rosh Chodesh Adar. Following R. Yitzchak Nafcha (some read this name as Nappacha), he states that, when Adar 1 coincides with Shabbat, we take three Torahs out: one for the weekly portion, one for Rosh Chodesh, and one for the "When you take count" portion. For some reason the Gemara notes that this same rabbi notes similarly that, when Rosh Chodesh Tevet coincides with Shabbat, we take out three Torahs: one for the weekly portion, one for Rosh Chodesh, and one for Chanukka. Do we really need both teachings here? Wouldn't mention of one of them enable us to infer the other? No, we need both because, for nuanced reasons, this accentuates R. Yitzchak Nafcha's support for Shmuel regarding the proper content of *Shekalim*.

The Gemara digresses at this point to discuss an apparent quandary with readings for Rosh Chodesh Tevet. Again there is some back-and-forth about the Chanukka reading and Rosh Chodesh reading, but the Gemara ultimately comes down on the side of prioritizing Rosh Chodesh's reading.

Possible issue with the *Shekalim* reading: if the regular time for this reading happened to coincide with a Shabbat on which we ordinarily would read the preceding passage in the Torah (*Exodus* 27.20–30.10). R. Yitzchak Nafcha states that six people read from that earlier portion right up to the beginning of the portion Shmuel taught for *Shekalim*. Then, a seventh person reads *Exodus* 30.11–16 which immediately follows. Abaye makes the point that

30a

people might assume that the weekly portion ends with these verses from *Exodus* and not realize they've just read *Shekalim*. Abaye now clarifies what he proposes: six people are called to the Torah to read through *Exodus* 30.16 and a seventh is then called to repeat *Exodus* 30.11–16, the *Shekalim* portion. R. Yitzchak Nafcha has a problem with repeating those verses, as he believes once should do it. One possible resolution is to read the special *Shekalim* verses on successive Shabbats, though others worry that a second reading of it would be out of order in the regular cycle. Abaye now offers another proposal that might do the trick: six readers cover *Exodus* 30.11 through 34.35, and a seventh then rereads 30.11–16. Another *baraita* comes to the rescue in support of Abaye.

The Mishna mentioned that, if Adar 1 coincides with a weekday, the reading of the *Shekalim* verses are pushed back to the previous Shabbat. OK, and if it coincides with a Friday, Rav says stay the course: previous Shabbat. Shmuel, though, says we read it on the Shabbat immediately following. Rav claims that, if we wait until Adar 2 (Shabbat, in Shmuel ruling), that cuts some time off the necessary two weeks allotted for the moneychangers to take up their positions before collecting the half-*shekel*. Shmuel rebuts this by demonstrating that, effectively, no time will be lost.

The Gemara now goes back-and-forth on this issue. When the Mishna mentions Rosh Chodesh Adar coming "during the week," does this mean literally in the middle of the week, or does any time not Shabbat count as "during"? Shmuel even suggests we change the text of the Mishna to fit his reading. The Gemara indicates that this Rav Shmuel debate actually reflects an earlier one between R. Yehuda ha-Nasi and R. Shimon ben Elazar. Ultimately, although not stated explicitly in the Gemara, Rav's view wins this round.

The Gemara seems to move on to a discussion of Purim (but not for long), and it wonders what we do with the *Zachor* portion, ordinarily read on the second Shabbat of Adar, if Purim coincides with the eve of Shabbat. Rav: move *Zachor* to the previous Shabbat. Shmuel: read it on the next Shabbat, Adar 15. Rav supports his position because he wants this "commemoration" (as he interprets *Zachor*) to come before the "observance" of the holiday of Purim, in alignment with *Megilla* 9.28, the verse now being cited for at least the eighth time in this tractate. Shmuel retorts that walled cities will be "observing" the holiday on Adar 15, meaning that both commemoration and observance occur at the same time. As with the previous

What about when Purim coincides with Shabbat itself? Rav Huna notes that we read *Zachor* (according to all parties) not on the previous Shabbat, but on Purim-Shabbat itself. Rav Nachman demurs, saying that the debate here has not as yet been resolved. He claims that Rav would still claim it should be read on the previous Shabbat, and the Gemara finds support for Rav's making this argument.

The Mishna noted that on the third Shabbat we read the *Para Aduma* portion, and this would be the Shabbat closest and after Purim itself. R. Chama son of R. Chanina claims that *Para Aduma* is read on Shabbat that comes close to Rosh Chodesh Nisan. Somehow a *baraita* resolves this dispute to satisfy both sides.

The reading for the fourth Shabbat of this sequence is "This month is for you." Rather than go into a detailed rehearsal of debate over the timing for this reading, the Gemara cites a lengthy *baraita* trying to go over all the details of the four special portions. It outlines which Torah portions are read on each of these four Shabbats and which additional selections as well.

30b

By the fourth Shabbat we are already into the week in which Rosh Chodesh Nisan occurs. And, from the fifth Shabbat, we return to the regular week-by-week order of things. The Gemara, as if stunned by the complications raised by these four special portions in Adar, asks what is meant by "regular." R. Ammi answers that, obviously, the regular cycle of weekly Torah portions, though R. Yirmeya suggests that instead it means the regular sequence of readings from the Prophets.

This one doesn't seem so terribly difficult to settle. Abaye likes R. Ammi's position, as it strikes him as more logical in light of how we deal with other interruptions in the ordinary sequence of weekly readings and what we do afterward when we return to the regular order. This return to normalcy not only concerns Shabbat readings but weekday ones as well, and there is no regular sequence of weekday readings from the Prophets. R. Yirmeya's position requires a little quick thinking, but it is quickly undermined from another angle. The example comes from a detailed discussion of behavior on a fast day, but basically Abaye's argument wins the day.

We now turn to the last Mishna in this tractate, a fairly long one which will not finish until the next *daf*. After the last Mishna's extended discussion of the "four portions" and their attendant readings, this Mishna details all the readings for all holidays and other special occurrences. Some of these are no longer extant, as we shall see shortly. The Mishna often, though not always, mentions the beginning of the required reading. We start with Passover when we read from *Leviticus* 22.27; on Shavuot we read from *Deuteronomy*

15.19–16.17; on Rosh Hashana we read from *Numbers* 29.1–9; on Yom Kippur we read from *Leviticus* 16.1–34; on the first day of Sukkot we read *Leviticus* 22.26–23.44 and on the rest of this holiday we read from *Numbers* 29.12–32; on Chanukka we read from *Numbers* 7; on Purim we read from *Exodus* 17.8–16; on new moons we read from *Numbers* 28.1–16; on days on which the changing of the weekly group responsible for Temple work, we read from the beginning of *Genesis*; and on fast days we read

31a

from *Leviticus* 26.3–46 (the blessings and curses). The curses are to be recited without a break—one person is called to the Torah and he reads the whole passage. On Monday and Thursday of regular weeks, as well as during the afternoon service of the previous Shabbat, we follow the regular schedule of Torah portions (for the coming Shabbat). These readings do not influence the allotted passages to be read on Shabbat. The Mishna ends with a definitive statement from *Leviticus* (23.44): "And Moses proclaimed to the children of Israel the festivals of God." This is meant to clarify that it is not a choice but a duty to read every single portion in its proper time.

The Gemara sets off with a long *baraita* which covers holidays cited in the Mishna and fills in information on holidays not mentioned in the Mishna and their respective readings from Torah. Thus, on Passover we read the Torah portion noted in the Mishna, and the Gemara adds that the Prophets selection comes from *Joshua* 5.2–6.27 (although current practice, both among Ashkenazim and Sefardim, differs). The Gemara also notes that, while the custom in the Land of Israel is to celebrate the first day, in the Diaspora the first two days are celebrated. On that second day, we read a different additional passage, *II Kings* 23.1–9 and 23.21–25. For the rest of this long holiday, we select Torah passages concerned with the topic of Passover. That's not quite good enough for the Gemara, and Rav Pappa is more specific with a number of possible suggestions. Abaye also has a series of suggestions which he claims is a practice followed by everyone everywhere.

For the holiday of Shavuot, the *baraita* has us reading *Habakkuk* 2.20–3.19 from the Prophets. Other authorities have a different Torah reading for Shavuot (*Exodus* 19.1–20.23). For a reading from the Prophets, it gives *Ezekiel* 1.1–28, 3.12 about the *Merkava* or heavenly chariot. Moving to Rosh Hashana, our Torah reading is as indicated in the Mishna, and the Prophets reading is from *Jeremiah* (31.2–20); again, an alternate possibility raised by other authorities is *Genesis* 21.1–34 for the Torah, and *I Samuel* 1.1–2.10 for the additional reading (from the story of Hannah). As a two-day holiday, same additional reading on day two, but the Torah reading that day should be *Genesis* 22.1–24.

On Yom Kippur the Torah reading is stated in the Mishna, and the Prophets reading comes from the book of *Isaiah* (57.14–58.14). For the afternoon service on Yom Kippur, there is a special Torah reading from *Leviticus* (18.1–30) followed by a reading of the book of *Jonah* in its entirety. The Gemara sticks in an odd exposition from R. Yochanan here pointing to the juxtaposition of God's power followed immediately by his humility in each of three parts of Tanakh, curiously anthropomorphizing to say the least.

Then comes Sukkot, another multi-day holiday, and on its first day we read *Leviticus* 22.26–23.44 for the Torah and *Zechariah* 14.1–21 for the Prophets. For the second day, same Torah reading and *I Kings* 8.2–21 for the additional reading. The Gemara goes on to the other days of Sukkot; on the last day, Shemini Atzeret, we read *Deuteronomy* 15.19–16.17, as the Mishna indicated, from the Torah and add the immediately preceding verses 14.22–15.18, with an additional reading from *I Kings* 8.54–9.1. In the Diaspora, there is a second day of Shemini Atzeret (aka Simchat Torah), and we read *Deuteronomy* 33.1–34.12, followed by *I Kings* 8.22–53. Should a Shabbat coincide with any of the intermediate days of Sukkot (or, for that matter, Passover), Rav Huna teaches that we read *Exodus* 33.12–34.26; from the Prophets, *Ezekiel* 37.1–14 for Passover and *Ezekiel* 38.18–39.16 for Sukkot.

On Chanukka, we read from chapter seven of *Numbers* from the Torah and *Zechariah* 2.14–4.7 from the Prophets. What happens if Chanukka's eight days cover two Shabbats (days one and eight)? In that eventuality, for the first one we read the designated *Zechariah* passage, and for the second one we read *I Kings* 8.40–50. The Mishna dealt with Purim and Rosh Chodesh, but the Gemara now asks about what we should do in the eventuality that Rosh Chodesh coincides with Shabbat. For a Prophets reading, it designates *Isaiah* 66.1–24; if it coincides with a Sunday, then on the preceding day of Shabbat, we read *I Samuel* 20.18–42 for the additional reading. Rav Huna adds some further data:

31b

If Rosh Chodesh for the month of Av coincides with Shabbat, our additional reading begins with *Isaiah* 1.14 (although this is not current practice).

More to come on the post-Torah additional readings for special days. On the Ninth of Av, Rav states that we read *Isaiah* 1.21 and subsequent verses. Torah reading for that day? Unsurprisingly, this arguably being the saddest day on the Jewish calendar, it's the curses verses in *Leviticus* (26.14–46). R. Natan bar Yosef suggests a passage from *Numbers* (14.11 and following), while others suggest *Numbers* 14.27 and following. Abaye notes that the current practice (in his day) was to read *Deuteronomy* 4.25–40 from the Torah and *Jeremiah* 8.13–9.23 from the Prophets.

The Mishna noted above that, on days when the weekly groups responsible for Temple work exchange places, our Torah reading comes from *Genesis*. This leads R. Ammi into a discussion, perhaps exaggerating, that these men and their offerings are the basis for God's covenant regarding heaven and earth. R. Ammi goes even further now to identify His covenant with these offerings. He bases this on a reading of the passages in *Genesis* in which Abraham has an exchange with God, which leads to a extra-Biblical and entirely constructed exchange in which Abraham extracts from God a promise to forgive the Jewish people their sins—even after the destruction of the Temple, which of course was many centuries in the future. This takes some considerable, heroic work on R. Ammi's part, but he appears to make it work.

The Mishna continued with fast days other than the Ninth of Av. How do we know to read the passage of blessings and curses on these days? R. Chiyya bar Gamda (in R. Ammi's name) cites *Proverbs* 3.11 which enjoins us to pay attention to God's reprimand. Reish Lakish leads the way into a lengthy digression on reading the curses, especially those in *Deuteronomy*. But, that only leads to further discussion of the difference of reading the curses in *Leviticus*.

The Gemara now segues to a *baraita* concerning the outline of weekly Torah readings. R. Meir states as follows: Where each weekly Shabbat portion of Torah finishes is the point where we start reading on that Shabbat's afternoon reading (which is the beginning of the following week's Torah portion). When the Shabbat afternoon reading ends is the beginning of Monday morning's reading; same pattern for MondayThursday, and for Thursdaynext Shabbat. R. Yehuda agrees about the reading for Shabbat afternoon, but he claims the readings on both Monday and Thursday come from the start of the following Shabbat's portion. R. Zeira states the latter pattern as *halacha*. Why didn't R. Zeira state his ruling as being in agreement with R. Yehuda?

32a

Simple: Some people confuse or switch the names of R. Meir and R. Yehuda, and in so doing the position laid out by R. Yehuda will be misconstrued. So. R. Zeira simply restated it and claimed it to be *halacha*.

For regular shul-goers, this next discussion should be very interesting, as the Gemara cites a *baraita* that lays out the proper formula for calling someone up to read Torah in a public setting. (1) The person called unscrolls the Torah and locates the point at which he will begin reading; (2) he then scrolls it back closed and invokes the proper blessing before reading; (3) he next re-opens the Torah scroll and proceeds to read. That's at least R. Meir's assessment, but R. Yehuda offers a slight variation: no need to close the Torah scroll when invoking the blessing. (While we generally follow R. Meir nowadays, there is no mention here of a blessing after the reading which is standard practice.)

So, why does R. Meir require we close the Torah before the blessing? In a parallel argument, Ulla claimed that, when Torah readings are immediately followed by Aramaic translation (*targum*), the reader of the Hebrew text must close the scroll, because one wouldn't want the congregation to think that the translation was actually written in the Torah scroll itself. Similarly, one wouldn't want anyone to think the blessings were transcribed there. What would be R. Yehuda's disagreement with Ulla's reasoning? He basically argues that it is well known that the blessings are not written in the Torah, but that is not the case with the translation, especially inasmuch as most people would never have actually seen the inside of a Torah scroll. The *halacha* follows R. Yehuda, according to R. Zeira (in Rav Matna's name), even though R. Yehuda would prefer rolling the Torah up before blessing it (just not absolutely necessary).

We move next to the proper manner for closing up a Torah scroll. In the name of R. Yochanan, R. Shefatya states that when rolling it closed, one must do so on a seam joining one piece of parchment to the next. Also, when trying to find a specific sheet of parchment, one need roll from the cylinder further from him, and when tightening a scroll, one need do so from the cylinder closer to one. If ten men (a *minyan*) are present for a Torah reading (as there must be at a minimum), the most distinguished is accorded the distinction of rolling the Torah scroll back together. R. Yehoshua ben Levi claims that just rolling the Torah back together affords the man who does this an honor the equal of any of those who read from it.

As we have seen it do more than once, the Gemara digresses to introduce several more rulings from R. Shefatya (in R. Yochanan's name). Back on *daf* 3a, we introduced the *bat kol* (Heavenly Voice), or a voice that rings out from the heavens, which oftentimes the rabbis instruct us to ignore (and make up our own minds rather than listen to a disembodied voice), but R. Shefatya cites *Isaiah* (30.21) to suggest we might on occasion listen to such a call from above. The Gemara quickly delimits this: one may listen but only if it's a male voice in the city or a female voice in the fields—because one would not expect such "voices" in those places—and the "voice" must only say: "yes, yes" or "no, no."

Another from R. Shefatya states that one must chant Torah with the proper cantillation and recite Mishna (from memory) with a proper tune. Failure to do so he deems worthy of condemnation (citing *Ezekiel* 20.25). Abaye thinks this denunciation over the top. Just because someone fails to have musical talent does not warrant such a rebuke.

R. Parnach, from whom we rarely hear in the Talmud, states in the name of R. Yochanan that one must never touch a Torah scroll with one's bare hands—or one will be buried without proper shrouds (bare). The Gemara thinks this is over the top and suggests that the burial of such a deviant person should be without proper *mitzvot* (bare in that sense). Even this strikes the Gemara as possibly too severe, and Abaye suggests that "bare" should mean only that the incident of grabbing the Torah scroll barehanded should not be counted in this person life record.

Tractate *Megilla* closes on a glorious note, citing our Mishna which states that "Moses proclaimed to the children of Israel the festivals of God." We are thus enjoined to read each of the proper holiday portions of Torah and Prophets and Writings at the proper time. A *baraita* tells us that Moses went further, that we should discuss the implications and laws of each of our festivals as part of the commemoration at their appointed times.

Thus ends Chapter Four and tractate *Megilla* itself. "Hadran," we shall return to you again, the traditional concluding phrase when one completes a chapter or an entire tractate of the Talmud.

Glossary of Selected Terms

Amora (pl. *Amoraim*): scholars from Babylonia and the Land of Israel who commented on and discussed the law, ca. 200–500 C.E., and whose debates constitute the bulk of the Gemara

bama (pl. *bamot*): a private altar allowed only at certain times when the Temple or Tabernacle was not in existence

baraita (pl. *baraitot*): oral laws not codified in the Mishnah and with slightly less authority

bat kol: Heavenly Voice

brit mila: covenant of circumcision

daf (pl. *dapim*): a Talmudic folio page, recto "a" and verso "b"

egla arufa: calf decapitated as part of the ritual following the discovery of a corpse whose murderer is unknown (see *Deuteronomy* 21:1–9 for details)

Gemara: collected commentary, discussions, and debates on the Mishna

gezera shava (pl. *gezerot shavot*): argument by analogy; when a word appears in two, sometimes three, separate places in the Hebrew Bible, the laws and meanings surrounding one may apply to the other(s) as well

H.: Hebrew

halacha: the legal portions of the Mishna

karet: a punishment, usually of premature death, administered by God

kometz: flour scooped with the middle three fingers of the right hand for *mincha* offering (see *kemitza*)

kemitza: extraction of the flour offering using the middle fingers of the right hand

kilayim: grains or vegetables grown in a vineyard; forbidden mixture; applies as well to prohibited crossbreeding of animals and mixtures of linen and wool

kohen (pl. *kohanim*): priests, the priestly class

maaser: tithe

metzora: someone afflicted with the skin ailment known as *tzaraat*, often "translated" as leprosy; can also be used to describe an "affliction" affecting the walls of buildings

meturgeman: "translator," the person rendering Biblical text as read from the synagogue podium into Aramaic (see *targum* below)

mezuza (pl. *mezuzot*): small box containing parchment inscribed with certain biblical Hebrew verses affixed to doorposts

mikve: ritual bath for purification of various kinds of impurities

Mishna (pl. Mishnayot): collection in six "orders" and numerous tractates of the laws of the Torah; also, the individual rulings in each Talmudic tractate

mitzvah (pl. *mitzvot*): commandment, good deed

Nasi (pl. *Nesiim*): prince, head of the Great Sanhedrin; head of one of the twelve tribes

R.: rabbi

Sanhedrin: assembly of 20–23 judges of most communities; Great Sanhedrin of 71 judges served as a Supreme Court

Shechina: divine presence

sotah: suspected adulteress who must drink the "bitter waters" to establish her innocence

Talmud (Bavli): Mishna combined with the Gemara of the rabbis and scholars primarily in Babylonia

Talmud (Yerushalmi): Mishna combined with the Gemara of the rabbis and scholars primarily in the Land of Israel

Tanna (pl. Tannaim): commentators of the Mishna, ca. 70–200 C.E.

Tanna Kamma: anonymous first voice of a Mishnah or *baraita*

targum: translation of Scripture into Aramaic, the lingua franca among Jews in the era of the Talmud

tefillin: "phylacteries," black boxes with long straps, containing sacred textual passages, typically worn by observant men during morning prayers, one for the head and one for the arm

tzaraat: (see metzora)

zav: a state of impurity due to seminal emissions requiring various procedures to regain ritual purity

zava: a woman whose menstrual bleeding lasts for three days in a row beyond the normative seven-day period

General Index

Aaron, 33, 36, 51, 53, 73, 105, 106
Abaye, 23, 26–27, 59, 76–77, 79, 89, 95–96, 99–101, 103, 111, 115–16, 122, 125–27, 129, 131
Abraham, 36, 51, 71, 105, 129
Achashverosh, King (Xerxes I), ix, 4, 22, 35–43, 46–51, 55, 57–58, 60–64, 66, 79
Achav, 37
I Adar, 20–21, 23
II Adar, 20–21, 23
Adar 10: 11
Adar 11: 1–3, 11
Adar 12: 1–2
Adar 13: 1, 3, 12
Adar 14: 1–4, 10–14, 16–17, 70, 78–79
Adar 15: 1–5, 9, 10, 11, 12–14, 16, 70, 78, 125
Agag, King, 36
aggada, 1
Amatzya, 33
Amnon, 105–6
Ashurit script, 27–29, 69, 78
Avigail, 51–52, 55
Avihu, 33
Avshalom, 106
Azarya, 34, 40, 44

Bar Chavu, 77

Bar Kappara, 113
baraita (pl. *baraitot*), 11–13, 15, 16, 22, 25, 27–30, 32, 33, 35, 36, 39, 42–43, 45, 48, 50, 51, 54, 55, 58, 62, 65, 67, 70–71, 74–77, 79, 82, 86, 88–89, 91, 93–97, 99–102, 104–6, 110–11, 114–18, 120–23, 125–27, 129, 131
Baruch, 54
Bathsheba, 52, 94
Belshatzar, King (Belshazzar), 38, 41–42
Ben Azzai, 45
Benjamin, 16, 43–44, 63–64, 106, 111
Bigtan, 22, 47–48, 57, 60
Bilhah, 104
birkat hakohanim, 73, 96, 100–102, 105–6, 118

Chaggai, 7
Chanamel, 54
Chananya, 34, 40, 44
Chanukka, 123
Charbona, 64
Chilkiya, 54
Chizkiya (Hezekiah), 16
Chonyo, 31
Chulda, 51, 53–54
Cyrus, King (Koresh), 37–39

Daniel, 7, 55–56
Darius, King (Daryavesh, the Mede), 37–39
David, King, 33, 36, 43, 52, 56, 72–73, 90, 105–6
Deborah, 51–53

Eli, 53
Elijah, 59, 81
Elkana, 51
Ephraim, 63
Esau, 18–19, 36, 119
Esther, ix, 10, 21–23, 32, 35, 45–48, 51, 53, 55–58, 59–60, 63, 66, 78, 79, 80
Evil Merodach, 38–39
Ezra, 32, 54–55, 66, 96

Gabriel, 42
gezera shava, 74, 78, 85, 86, 98
Golden Calf, 104–6

halacha, 3, 20, 29, 75–77, 80, 92, 121, 129–30
Haman, ix, 10, 22–23, 32, 34–36, 40–41, 43, 48, 49–51, 55, 57–66, 70, 79–80
Hannah, 51–53, 127
Hatach, 55
Heavenly Voice (*bat kol*), 6–7, 130
Hillel, 21
Hillel II, 1
Hitler, Adolf, ix

Isaac, 19, 56, 67, 71
Ishmael, 67

Jacob, 18–19, 33, 47, 64–67, 71, 94
Joseph, 47, 64–65, 67, 94
Joshua, 1, 4, 8, 9–10, 15–16, 32, 54–54, 94
Judah, 10, 33, 44, 53, 63, 105, 110

kal vachomer, 8

Laban, 47, 67

Leah, 47
Levi bar Shmuel, 80

Machseya, 54
Malachi, 7, 54–55
Mar Zutra, 113, 119
Mari bar Mar, 23
Memuchan, 43, 63
Men of the Great Assembly, 2, 71, 73, 103
Menashe, 63
Merkava, ix, 101, 105, 127
meturgeman, 76, 89, 97, 99, 104
mezuza (pl. *mezuzot*), 27, 28, 77, 112
Michal, 55
minyan, 9, 14, 97–98, 117, 130
Miriam, 51–53
Mishael, 34, 40, 44
Molech, 103–4
Mordechai, ix, 2, 21–23, 35, 41, 43–49, 54–57, 59–66, 79, 80
Moses, 5, 29, 33, 36, 44–45, 48–49, 51, 58, 74, 80, 81, 86, 88, 91, 102, 105, 127, 131

Naval, 52
Nehemiah, 6
Neriya, 54
Nevuchadnetzar, King, 34–40, 114
Ninth of Av (Tisha b'Av), 14–15, 93, 129

Og, king of Bashan, 58
Onkeles, 6

Passover, 3, 15, 20, 49, 49, 50, 56, 86, 93, 93, 124, 127, 128
Pharaoh, 34–35, 44, 48, 50, 51, 58, 67
prophets, x, 5–7, 27, 28, 33, 87–89, 93, 96–97, 99–100, 104, 1–5, 106, 114, 126–29, 131
Ptolemy, King, 28
Purim, ix-x. 2–5, 8–10, 13–16, 20–23, 32, 35–36, 45, 47, 49–51, 56, 66, 74–75, 78–80, 83, 123, 124–28

General Index

Reuben, 104, 106
R. Abba, 49, 76
R. Abba bar Kahana, 34, 50
R. Abba bar Zavda, 15
R. Abbahu, 18, 29, 66, 77, 88, 122
R. Acha bar Yaakov, 70, 72, 74
R. Aleksandri, 72
R. Ammi, 126, 129
R. Assi, 66
R. Akiva, 22, 95, 122
R. Binyamin bar Yefet, 64–65
R. Chanan, 41
R. Chanina, 10, 15, 36, 56, 88, 103, 126
R. Chanina bar Pappa, 34
R. Chanina ben Gamliel, 106
R. Chanina (Chananya?) Kara, 91
R. Chananya ben Gamliel, 24
R. Chelbo, 10, 13, 73, 80, 122
R. Chiyya, 36
R. Chiyya bar Abba, 5–7, 10, 29, 46–47, 80, 81, 98
R. Chiyya bar Avin, 20, 50
R. Chiyya bar Gamda, 129
R. Eina the Elder, 53–54
R. Elazar, 9, 15, 20, 34–35, 41, 46–47, 56, 63–65, 74, 82, 94, 119, 122
R. Elazar bar Tsadok, 111
R. Elazar ben Azarya, 86
R. Elazar ben Shamua, 118
R. Elazar Hakapar, 122
R. Eliezer, 6, 25, 31–32, 58, 59, 65, 105, 106, 110
R. Eliezer bar Yose (R. Eliezer son of R. Yose), 9, 20–22
R. Eliezer ha-Modai, 59
R. Levi, 33, 36, 43, 57, 90
R. Meir, 21–22, 29–30, 41, 45, 48, 59, 77–80, 82, 115–17, 129–30
R. Menachem bar Yose, 110
R. Muna, 76
R. Natan bar Yosef, 128
R. Nechemya, 40, 45, 59
R. Nechunya ben Hakkana, 24, 119
R. Oshaaya, 23
R. Parnach, 131

R. Preida, 118–19
R. Shefatya, 130
R. Sheila, 53
R. Shimi, 89
R. Shimon, 21, 25, 30
R. Shimon ben Elazar, 77, 106, 125
R. Shimon ben Menasya, 21, 59
R. Shimon ben Pazi, 44
R. Shimon ben Yochai, 19, 40, 79–80, 96, 122
R. Tanchum, 60, 66, 91
R. Yehoshua, 6, 32, 34, 58, 120
R. Yehoshua ben Korcha, 4–5, 50, 54–55, 59, 119–20
R. Yehoshua ben Levi, 8–10, 44–45, 83, 90–91, 101, 113–14, 121, 130
R. Yehuda, 3, 14, 24, 40, 45, 46, 59, 74, 76, 78–83, 89, 100–1, 105, 110, 117, 119, 120–21, 129, 130
R. Yehuda bar Ilai, 63
R. Yehuda ha-Nasi (Rabbi Judah the Prince), 7, 8, 11–13, 15–16, 23, 30, 70–71, 75, 83, 94, 119–20, 125
R. Yehuda Nesia, 23
R. Yirmeya, 5–7, 9, 17, 47, 55, 58, 77, 126
R. Yirmeya bar Abba, 76, 96
R. Yishmael, 41, 95, 104
R. Yishmael son of R. Yose, 32
R. Yitzchak, 18–19, 31, 51, 55, 122
R. Yitzchak bar Avdimi, 125
R. Yitzchak bar Nachamani, 96
R. Yitzchak Nafcha (Nappacha), 124–25
R. Yochanan, 2–3, 17–20, 24, 29, 34–36, 44, 46–48, 53, 58, 62, 65, 71, 74, 77, 79–81, 88, 90, 97–98, 101, 110, 114–18, 128, 130, 131
R. Yonatan, 6, 33–34, 110
R. Yose, 12, 20–21, 29–30, 32, 59, 78–82, 85, 93, 101
R. Yose bar Avin, 103
R. Yose bar Chanina, 7–8, 18, 39–40, 42
R. Yose bar Zevida, 103
R. Yose ben Durmaskit, 22
R. Yosef ben Ulam, 30

R. Zakkai, 118
R. Zeira, 17–18, 23, 84, 104, 119–21, 129–30
Rabba, 10, 16–17, 23, 59, 66, 70, 92, 103, 110
Rabba bar Avuha, 59
Rabba bar bar Chana, 18, 44, 73, 75, 77–78, 110, 115
Rabba bar Ofran, 34, 58
Rabba bar Shimi, 100
Rabba son of Rava. *See* Rabba
Rabban Gamliel, 59, 71, 88
Rabban Shimon ben Gamliel, 20–21, 27–29, 75, 115, 124
Rachav, 54–55
Rachel, 33, 47
Rafram, 121
Rami bar Abba, 60, 111
Rav, 13–14, 35–36, 39–41, 43, 46, 51, 53, 55–56, 64, 66, 74–75, 76, 77, 80, 88, 91–92, 94, 118, 122, 124–26, 129, 130
Rav Acha, 45, 112–13
Rav Acha bar Yaakov, 113
Rav Acha son of Rav Ika, 106
Rav Acha son of Rava, 121
Rav Ada bar Matna, 121
Rav Ashi, 3, 15, 32, 33, 35, 77, 89, 93, 106, 110–11, 118, 121
Rav Assi, 14, 16, 89, 99, 101, 121
Rav Avya, 70
Rav Bivi, 76
Rav Chama bar Gurya, 77, 80
Rav Chana bar Chanilai, 119
Rav Chananel, 77
Rav Chisda, 5, 30, 37, 39, 57, 77, 111, 121
Rav Chiyya bar Avin, 95
Rav Dimi, 74
Rav Dimi bar Yitzchak, 34
Rav Huna, 13, 46, 80, 92, 96, 101, 111, 116, 118–19, 126, 128
Rav Huna bar Manoach, 106
Rav Kahana, 43, 76
Rav Mari, 31

Rav Matna, 35, 81, 130
Rav Nachman bar Yitzchak, 18, 22, 24, 28, 35, 39, 51, 53–55, 60, 70, 106, 117, 122, 126
Rav Oshaya, 15, 23
Rav Pappa, 20, 26, 28, 89, 100, 102, 104, 111, 113, 127,
Rav Shemen bar Abba, 2–3
Rav Sheshet, 62, 89, 116, 121–22
Rav Shmuel, 40, 91, 125
Rav Shmuel bar Abba, 97
Rav Shmuel bar Marta, 66
Rav Shmuel bar Nachmani, 3, 33–34, 110
Rav Shmuel bar Unya, 8
Rav Shmuel bar Yehuda, 21
Rav Yosef, 13, 18, 23, 30, 35, 66, 70, 76, 90, 92, 96, 104
Rav Yehuda, 21, 80, 89, 96
Rava, 3, 5, 8, 15, 16, 17, 22–23, 25, 26–27, 31, 35, 37, 39, 41–42, 45, 48–49, 51, 59–60, 70, 72, 74, 78–80, 83, 88–92, 95, 97, 102, 104, 111–13, 115–16, 119, 121, 122
Ravina, 22, 32, 75, 111–12, 121
Reish Lakish, 18, 35, 50, 121, 129
Rosh Chodesh, 87, 90–91, 93, 123–26, 128
Rosh Hashana, xi, 93, 127

Sancheriv (Sennacherib), 37
Sarah, 51, 55, 56
Saul, King, 36, 47, 52
Seraya, 54
Shabbat, 1–2, 10, 12–15, 23–24, 42, 45, 68n4, 87–89, 94–95, 96, 97, 123–29
Shallum, 54
Shammai, 21
Shapiro, Rabbi Meir, xi
Shechina, 58, 122
Shemini Atzeret, 128
Shimon Hapakuli, 71, 73
Shimon ha-Tzaddik, 31
Shimshai, 60

Shmuel, 14, 21–22, 35–37, 39, 40–41, 46, 55–56, 74–76, 80, 89, 91–92, 117, 124–25
Shushan, 1, 4–5, 35, 37, 39–40, 47, 56, 61, 65
Simchat Torah, 128
Solomon, King, 21, 33, 37, 52
Sukkot, 15, 84, 127–28

Tabernacle, 30–31, 33, 52, 64
Tamar, 33, 104–6
Tanakh, 27, 40, 89, 99, 128
targum, 6–7, 69, 130
tefillin, 27–28, 65, 77, 102, 112, 120
Teresh, 22, 47–48, 57, 60
Torah, ix, x, 4–5, 6–9, 18, 19–20, 26, 27, 28, 29, 35–36, 41, 42, 44–45, 50–51, 57, 64–66, 71, 77, 80, 81, 85, 87, 88, 89–97, 99–103, 105–6, 109, 112–15, 117–31
Tower of Babel, 29, 33
tsaraat, 26, 42, 110

Ula Biraa, 10

Ulla, 19, 54, 94, 97, 130
Ulla bar Rav, 90, 130

Vaizata, 65
Vashti, Queen, 23, 34, 38, 41–42, 55, 63, 80

writings, x, 5–6, 27, 28, 33, 89, 99, 114, 131

Yael, 55
Yehoyachin, King, 38
Yehu, 52
Yiska, 51
Yom Kippur, 24, 29, 84, 85, 87–88, 94–96, 99, 123, 127–28
Yonatan ben Uziel, 6
Yoshiya, King, 53

Zechariah, 7, 96
Zeira, 17–18
Zeresh, 62
Zevulun, 17–18

Biblical and Rabbinic References Index

Berachot, 81

Chagiga, 67n1
I Chronicles, 9, 36, 44
II Chronicles, 36

Daniel, 6, 7, 37–38, 56
Deuteronomy, 5, 7, 18, 24, 28, 31, 34, 35, 49, 62, 65, 69, 70, 74, 81, 82, 85, 88, 101, 103, 105, 123, 126, 128, 129

Ecclesiastes, 15, 21, 34, 35
Esther (Scroll of Esther, *Megilla*), ix–x, 1–4, 7, 8–14, 15, 16, 20–23, 28, 32, 33–37, 39–43, 45–51, 53, 55–63, 65–66, 69–70, 74–84, 87–89, 96, 123–25, 131
Ethics of the Fathers, 2
Exodus, 24, 29, 34, 36, 37, 39, 44, 51, 74, 86, 104, 106, 123–25, 127, 128
Ezekiel, ix, 72, 101, 105, 106, 122, 127, 128, 130
Ezra, 34, 37, 38, 39

Genesis, 18, 28–29, 32, 33, 36, 51, 56, 63–65, 67, 83, 90, 91, 94, 104, 105, 127–28, 129

Habakkuk, 127

Hallel, 50–51, 70, 84, 89
Hosea, 73, 106

Isaiah, 19, 33–34, 39, 57, 71–73, 99, 107, 115, 128, 130

Jeremiah, 34, 38, 53, 54, 56, 59, 78, 97, 127, 129
Job, 45, 47, 74, 119
Joshua, 8, 17, 94, 127
Judges, 17, 52, 106
I Kings, 21, 33, 94, 128
II Kings, 53, 96, 114, 124, 127

Leviticus, 5, 9, 25, 26–27, 29, 32–33, 35–36, 73, 83, 84–85, 94, 98, 99, 103, 105, 113, 120, 126, 127, 128, 129

Menachot, 68n3, 85, 86

Nechemiah, 84, 96
Numbers, 7, 36, 83, 84, 85, 90, 96, 98, 105, 106, 123, 124, 127, 128–29

Proverbs, 19, 22, 35, 58–59, 62, 65, 117, 119, 129
Psalms, 19, 34, 35, 58, 63, 65, 70, 72, 73, 74, 84, 90, 122

Ruth, 21, 32

I Samuel, 36, 47, 51, 52, 59, 127, 128
II Samuel, 45, 105
Shekalim, 123–25
Shema, 7, 70–71, 81–82, 97, 98,
    100–101, 104
Shemone Esrei, 70–71, 73, 97,
    98, 100, 103

Song of Songs, 21
Sotah, 88

Yevamot, 54
Yoma, 99

Zechariah, 7, 18, 45, 128
Zephaniah, 18
Zevachim, 31, 68n2

About the Author

Joshua A. Fogel is professor of history at York University in Toronto (since 2005). He previously taught at Harvard University (1981–1988) and the University of California, Santa Barbara (1989–2005). He is the author, editor, or translator of seventy books. His major field of study is Chinese and Japanese history, but he retains an abiding interest in Jewish history as well. *The Whole Megilla* is his fifth volume on tractates of the Babylonian Talmud, and like the previous four, it follows (page by page) the text in an effort to make this difficult text comprehensible to modern, interested readers. Earlier works in East Asian studies include: *Maiden Voyage: The* Senzaimaru *and the Creation of Modern Sino-Japanese Relations*; and *A Friend in Deed: Lu Xun, Uchiyama Kanzō, and the Intellectual World of Shanghai on the Eve of War*.

www.ingramcontent.com/pod-product-compliance
Lightning Source LLC
Chambersburg PA
CBHW030122240426
43673CB00041B/1366